In this superb and em[...] Kendall demonstrates [...] tory, and personal experience what happens when the Word and the Spirit are severed, as well as when they are properly wedded in the lives of God's people. R. T. is certainly correct when he says that "we need *more* than the Bible. We need the Holy Spirit."

This book is a clarion call to the church of Jesus Christ to wake us up to the fact that we have all contributed to the divorce between the two. Where did we ever get the idea that any Christian could ever live without the infallible instruction of Scripture and the empowering ministry of the Spirit? Both those who have embraced Charismatic renewal and those who oppose it can benefit immensely from R. T.'s insights. I highly recommend it to all in both camps!

—SAM STORMS, PHD
BRIDGEWAY CHURCH,
OKLAHOMA CITY, OKLAHOMA
ENJOYING GOD MINISTRIES

This book contains a wealth of experience in God from a man who has preached the Word for over sixty years and has not slowed down. He has rubbed shoulders with famous scholars, great preachers, and powerful prophets. He confesses what it was like for him to preach the Word without the conscious presence of the Holy Spirit, and he tells the story of how the Spirit came to him and changed his life and his ministry. Most importantly he explains why he believes the church is heading for the greatest outpouring of the Holy Spirit since the days of the first apostles.

—JACK DEERE
BESTSELLING AUTHOR

There is such a deep stirring in the church for revival. We long to see God bring about an awakening in our day. But we wonder what we need to do. In this book R. T. Kendall shows us the pathway for revival in the church, through bringing together the Word and Spirit. Regardless of how long you've been following Jesus or leading in the church, the message of this book is convicting and powerful. It will help us position our hearts and churches for revival.

—KEVIN QUEEN
LEAD PASTOR, CROSS POINT CHURCH,
NASHVILLE, TENNESSEE

In Matthew 22:29 Jesus kindly corrects the Sadducees that had come to trick Him with a hypothetical situation. He says, "Your mistake is that you don't know the Scriptures, and you don't know the power of God" (NLT). I believe these words of Jesus can be applied to much of the church today where, sadly, there seems to be a dichotomy around these subjects. Either you belong to a church that emphasizes the Scriptures, or you belong to a church that emphasizes the power. I've been around both types of Christians: the ones who know Scripture but don't "know" or aren't "familiar" with the power of God; and pastors from the bush in Africa who have raised people from the dead (power) but don't know the Scriptures.

I believe that God, in these last days, is raising a standard in His church in that His people will be a people who know the Scriptures *and* the power of God.

R. T. Kendall's book is a call for the church to repent from an either/or mentality and embrace the whole Gospel message of the kingdom—the Word and the Spirit working together side by side.

—Jeff Dollar
Senior Pastor, Grace Center
Author, *Letting Go*
of the Need to Be Right

This is not just another book for R. T. Kendall to add to his long list; this is a call to get ready. *Word and Spirit* is a book to prepare the bride of Christ for her Groom. It brings the church to the place God always longed for it to be, that His holy Word and His Holy Spirit would be the center-piece before His coming. R. T. Kendall says that it's time for both of these things to come together, and when they do, there will be an explosion heard in the church. R. T. shows us that this has been God's desire and God's plan, but now we are given in R. T.'s newest book the how-to in moving forward.

—Tim Dilena
Lead Pastor, Our Savior's Church
Lafayette, Louisiana

WORD&
SPIRIT

WORD&
SPIRIT

R.T. KENDALL

CHARISMA
HOUSE

Visit the author's website at www.rtkendallministries.com and
RTKendall.com.

Library of Congress Cataloging-in-Publication Data:
An application to register this book for cataloging has been submitted
to the Library of Congress.
International Standard Book Number: 978-1-62999-649-3
E-book ISBN: 978-1-62999-650-9

Portions of this book were previously published as *The Word and
the Spirit* in the United Kingdom by Kingsway Publications, ISBN
0-85476-413-5, copyright © 1996, and in the United States by
Charisma House, ISBN 0-88419-544-9, copyright © 1998.

This publication is translated in Spanish under the title *La Palabra
y el Espíritu*, copyright © 2019 by R. T. Kendall, published by Casa
Creación, a Charisma Media company. All rights reserved.

19 20 21 22 23 — 987654321
Printed in the United States of America

But I would bring everything to the test of the Word and the Spirit. Not the Word only, but the Word and the Spirit. "God is a Spirit," said our Lord, "and they that worship him must worship him in spirit and in truth" (John 4:24). While it is never possible to have the Spirit without at least some measure of truth, it is, unfortunately, possible to have a shell of truth without the Spirit. Our hope is that we may have both the Spirit and the truth in fullest measure.

—A. W. TOZER, *GOD'S PURSUIT OF MAN*

I dedicate this book to a remarkable prayer warrior, Dr. Ann Allen Salter, a veterinarian from Mobile, Alabama. A specialist on all animals, especially doves, Dr. Salter has given great insight, not to mention prayer support, over the years.

TABLE OF CONTENTS

Acknowledgments

My deepest thanks to Marcos Perez, publisher and executive vice president of Charisma House, for his encouragement that I produce this book. Warmest thanks also to Joy Strang, who kindly read the manuscript and offered some needed suggestions. Also, thank you, Debbie Marrie, for editing this work, knowing how strongly I feel that my books are *not* verbally inspired by the Holy Spirit! Thank you, Mark Driscoll, for the insightful foreword you have provided for my book. Finally, thanks to my wife, Louise, for her patience and invaluable help.

I pray that God will bless everyone who reads this book with an ever-increasing hunger and thirst to know the Word better and receive more of the Holy Spirit.

—R. T. Kendall

FOREWORD

WHEN JESUS SAID the Holy Spirit was like the wind, He was teaching us that Christianity is a bit like sailing a boat. The powerful presence of the blowing wind fills a sail and drives a boat toward its destination. Without the wind a boat lacks all power, and rather than driving forward, remains lifeless, stuck, and dead in the water.

It is the steadiness of a rudder that keeps a boat on course, driving forward by harnessing and focusing all the power of the wind for a purpose. Without a rudder a boat has power but veers off course until it is lost, eventually crashing into rocks and sinking.

Some churches are sail churches, and some Christians are sail Christians. They are open to and filled by the powerful presence of the wind of the Spirit. They excel at such things as prayer and worship as they exercise power in spiritual war, driving the kingdom of God forward through the stormy seas of this dark and dying demonic world.

Some churches are rudder churches, and some Christians are rudder Christians. Like a rudder, they are focused on staying on course and not getting blown off course by every wind of false teaching. They excel at such things as doctrine and theology as they engage their mind in deep Bible study, seeking to follow God's directions obediently.

Sadly, sail churches and Christians and rudder churches and Christians often criticize one another rather than collaborating. The sails accuse the rudders of being dead, unspiritual, small-minded, powerless, and passionless. The rudders accuse the sails of being too emotional, off course, and dangerous.

In this significant book R. T. Kendall seeks to bring the wind of the Spirit and the rudder of the Word together in a way that all Christians and churches desperately need. He combines a theologian's mind, a pastor's heart, a worshipper's soul, and a grandfather's experience in a message that is timely because it is timeless. Today Christianity exists on a sea of trouble as the world grows darker and waves swell higher. More than ever we need the power of the Spirit focused by the truth of the Word so that we can safely get to the harbor Jesus has waiting for us. I highly recommend this book from a seasoned and steady captain who has spent his entire life faithfully at the helm.

—MARK DRISCOLL
FOUNDING SENIOR PASTOR, THE TRINITY CHURCH
AUTHOR OF *SPIRIT-FILLED JESUS*

INTRODUCTION

WOULD YOU LIKE to see the glory of God, genuine miracles, and the fear of the Lord return to the church? Would you like to see a return to the Gospel by which the cross of our Lord Jesus Christ is extolled and honored? Would you like to see people astonished by teaching and preaching as easily as signs and wonders move them?

Moreover, would you like to see the fear of God come upon nations? When a discouraged and backslidden Jacob returned to Bethel and got right with God, lo and behold, "a terror from God fell upon *the cities that were around them*" (Gen. 35:5, emphasis added). When King Jehoshaphat and the priests were right with God, "the fear of the LORD fell upon all the kingdoms of *the lands that were around Judah*" (2 Chron. 17:10, emphasis added).

The fear of God upon the early church had the same effect. Luke stated that "great fear came upon the whole church" and that "signs and wonders were regularly done...by the hands of the apostles" (Acts 5:11–12).

Much of the world has little or no respect for the church today, but the things mentioned above will return to the church and be witnessed by the world when the Word and the Spirit are at long last brought back together. What I have called a "silent divorce" between the Word and the Spirit will end in a glorious reconciliation.

It is coming soon.

I cannot think of anything that would honor God more or threaten Satan more than the Word and the Spirit coming together simultaneously, as was demonstrated in the Book of Acts. As long as these two remain separated to any degree, it becomes easier for the devil to keep the church from making a significant impact on the world.

When I say there has been a silent divorce between the Word and the Spirit, I mean that with many people today it has been one or the other. Some are well-acquainted with the Scriptures. They know their Bibles. They know their doctrine. They know their church history. They can detect heresy a mile away. I call these people Word people.

Meanwhile others emphasize the power of the Holy Spirit, some being well-acquainted with the raw power of God. They have experienced the infilling of the Holy Spirit. They have experienced His gifts. They have seen healings, even miracles. And they can detect dead orthodoxy a mile away. I call these people Spirit people.

There is nothing wrong with either emphasis. Each is exactly right. Take, for an example, those of us who represent the Reformed tradition, as I do. We say, "We must earnestly contend for the faith once delivered unto the saints. We must recover our Reformation heritage. We must return to the God of Jonathan Edwards and Charles Spurgeon. We must be sound in doctrine."

Or take another example, those who come from a Pentecostal or Charismatic perspective. They say, "We must recover apostolic power. The need of the day is for a renewal of the gifts of the Spirit. Signs and wonders were seen in the Book of Acts; we too must see them. What is needed is a demonstration of power."

My message in this book is this: the church generally will struggle on and on in its plea for God to restore the honor of His name until not one or the other, but *both*—the Scriptures and the power of God, the Word and the Spirit—coalesce simultaneously.

We are living at a time when the fear of God is mostly absent in the church, speaking generally. The world is not afraid of us or threatened by us but instead thumbs its nose at us while we are in a deep sleep. There is no sense of outrage anymore over conditions in society.

The advance of evil throughout the world is now so swift that we have watched standards of morality and decency degenerate before our eyes without it bothering us as it once might have. Until the fear of God returns to the church, men's ways will go "from bad to worse" (2 Tim. 3:13). This is because the church, according to Jesus, is "the salt of the earth." But He also said that if the salt loses its taste, "it is no longer good for anything except to be thrown out and trampled under people's feet" (Matt. 5:13).

I'm sorry—I wish it were not so, but this is precisely what the church is like in many parts of the world as I write these lines. The only thing that will bring the fear of God back to the church—aside from the pure Gospel of Christ—is for the Word of God and the Holy Spirit to come together in equal measure.

The day of Pentecost began with scoffing. After the Holy

Spirit fell on the 120 disciples, mockers said, "They are filled with new wine" (Acts 2:13). However, once the Word of God was preached through the power of the Spirit by Peter, cynicism turned to fear. As a result of Peter's preaching, they were "cut to the heart" and cried out, "What shall we do?" (v. 37). The residual fallout of that historic day was the fear of God: "Awe came upon every soul" (v. 43).

Shortly after that, Satan managed to get Ananias and Sapphira to lie to the Holy Spirit, but Peter—filled with Spirit—quickly discerned what was going on. He rebuked Ananias and Sapphira, and they dropped dead instantly. The fear of God remained at a very high level (Acts 5:1–11)—indeed, so much so that unbelievers "dared join them, but the people held them in high esteem" (v. 13).

As I said, it is my view that the fear of God will not return to the church until the Word and the Spirit come together again. The simultaneous combination will result in spontaneous combustion. The world will once again ask, "What shall we do?"

It is also my view that such a day is coming—and coming soon.

MY FIRST ENCOUNTER WITH WORD AND SPIRIT

As far as I know, the first Word and Spirit Conference took place at London's Wembley Conference Centre in October 1992. The conference was sponsored and organized by Beulah, an interdenominational group of churches in North London. Lyndon Bowring chaired the meetings, and Graham Kendrick led the worship at the celebration.

Graham introduced his song "Jesus, Restore to Us Again," which was written for the occasion and centers on the need for the Word and the Spirit to come together in the church.

One of my contributions at this conference was not an expository sermon but rather a statement. It is called "Isaac" in the final chapter of this book. The apostle Paul gave an allegory about Hagar and Ishmael and Sarah and Isaac. (See Galatians 4:21–23.) Paul did this in the context of showing the purpose and place of the Law. What I have done with the original account is to apply it prophetically to our day.

I believe that ancient history is repeating itself. In the same way that Abraham sincerely thought Ishmael was the promised son, many have believed the current Pentecostal/ Charismatic movement is *the* ultimate revival that God promised before the second coming. I question this. It is my view that a move of the Spirit far greater than any movement in church history—namely, "Isaac"—is coming. It will be a work of God more significant than anything heretofore seen—even in proportion to Isaac's greatness over Ishmael.

The church is on the brink of a post-Charismatic era of unprecedented glory. In my opinion it is the *same* as the midnight cry that we read about in the parable of the ten virgins (Matt. 25:1–13). It is when the Word and the Spirit come together as seen in the Book of Acts. Smith Wigglesworth (1859–1947) said much the same thing.

I believe "Isaac" will arrive suddenly without any further notice when the church is in a deep, deep spiritual sleep— expecting nothing. This is precisely where we are now. The church generally being in deep sleep is the most accurate description of the church at the present time. This wake-up call can happen at any moment, and it is coming very soon.

The question is: Are we ready for it?

PART I:
THE POWER OF
THE SPIRIT

Chapter One

CAN WE HAVE THE WORD WITHOUT THE SPIRIT?

For when the foolish took their lamps,
they took no oil with them.

—MATTHEW 25:3

I WAS THE PASTOR of Westminster Chapel for twenty-five years. It was a great honor, a great privilege; but I seldom saw the Holy Spirit move as I hoped. Not that we were barren. I baptized many people; we saw genuine conversions regularly. We even saw some people healed—not a lot, but a few that were genuine. In any case most people who came to Westminster came to hear the Word. It had become known as a "preaching center" during the ministries of G. Campbell Morgan (1863–1945) and Dr. D. Martyn Lloyd-Jones (1899–1981). Westminster Chapel was known for biblical preaching, especially expository preaching. I continued this tradition. A typical comment after a sermon was—even if it was a British courtesy—"Thank you for your word." That was what people came for; that was what they got: the Word.

I want to show in this chapter that we can have the Word without the Spirit, that is, the Word without the conscious presence of the Holy Spirit. To understand what I mean by this, you must first understand that there is a difference between the *conscious* presence of the Spirit and the *unconscious* presence of the Spirit.

When Paul said, "Our gospel came to you not only in word, but also in power and in the Holy Spirit" (1 Thess. 1:5), he implied that one *could* preach the Word without power and without the Holy Spirit. He meant that the *conscious* presence of God was manifest in Thessalonica. He said virtually the same thing to the Corinthians: "My speech and my message were not in plausible words of wisdom, but in demonstration of the Spirit and of power" (1 Cor. 2:4).

In both instances, Paul could testify to the *conscious* presence of the Spirit. Likewise, in both cases, Paul implies that he might have spoken in word only. But he didn't—at least not in those instances. The conscious presence of the Holy Spirit accompanied his preaching with power. He knew this was essential to effective preaching.

For this reason, he asked the Ephesians to pray for him that he be given "words" to proclaim "boldly" the Gospel (Eph. 6:19). *Words* comes from the Greek *logos*, which we will examine in more detail below. *Boldly* comes from *parresia*—which means "boldness" or "freedom in speaking."[1] It is what Peter had when he preached on the day of Pentecost (Acts 2:14–41). It was what Paul wanted the Ephesians to ask for in prayer. I am sure God answered their prayer, but if such freedom, boldness, or utterance came inevitably every time Paul stood up to preach, he would not have asked the Ephesians to pray for him as he did. He was not merely displaying humility by asking for their prayers; he knew that without the power of the Spirit giving him utterance and boldness, his efforts would be far less effective.

Most preachers will admit to the experience of preaching without liberty. It is not fun. Some will say, "Ah, but the Holy Spirit still blesses His Word—it will not return void." (See Isaiah 55:11.) True. I know what it is to preach without the feeling of liberty and still have people converted. At times my preaching felt like an utter failure to me, but I had people say to me, "How did you know I was there today?" So there is a *sense* in which the Spirit will always accompany the Word. It is the *unconscious* presence of the

Spirit at work in such situations, as I seek to show in my book *The Presence of God* (Charisma House). We should never underestimate the unconscious presence of the Holy Spirit.

Some teach that the Word and Spirit are invariably inseparable. They would say that Paul's statements about his own preaching with power prove this—as if this was the case every time he preached and that all who preach sound doctrine will have the same level of power he had. Many cessationists—those who believe that the miraculous ceased by God's decree a long time ago—want to make a big point of this. I don't mean to be unfair, but I suspect that some hold to this idea so they won't need to pray for an increased anointing.

One of the greatest privileges of my entire life was having a close relationship with Dr. Lloyd-Jones, the greatest preacher since Charles Spurgeon (1834–1892). He opened his home to me from the first day I became the pastor of Westminster Chapel. I was privileged not only to be tutored by him, but I got to know how his mind worked. I knew his heartbeat—his theological views, his political opinions, and the things that he loved most. I was surprised when one well-known cessationist openly criticized Dr. Lloyd-Jones for "chasing after the anointing." As a matter of fact Dr. Lloyd-Jones longed for a greater anointing on his preaching more than anything and urged all the ministers who attended the Westminster Fellowship to want the same thing. He always said, "I'm an eighteenth-century man [the age of John Wesley and George Whitefield] not a seventeenth-century man [the age of the Puritans]."

He insisted on being called "a Calvinistic Methodist." He embraced the sovereignty of God like historical Calvinists but admired the openness to the "immediate and direct witness of the Holy Spirit" that characterized the early Methodists. Many references to him—as in my book *Holy Fire* (Charisma House)—come from personal memory. Evan Roberts (1878–1951), the leading light of the Welsh Revival (1904–1905) was a Calvinistic Methodist. The early Methodists believed in the immediate and direct witness of the Holy Spirit—what they could consciously experience.

There is a sense in which the Word and Spirit are inseparable but not *consciously* inseparable. If you say that the Word and the Spirit are unconsciously inseparable, I would agree. First of all, we would not have the Old and New Testaments without the Spirit. The Holy Spirit wrote the Bible, as we will see in more detail later. However, it does not follow that the Spirit will always apply the Word. Sometimes the Holy Spirit applies the Word and sometimes, owing to His sovereign prerogative, He doesn't. A printed word on a billboard can quote a scripture. You see this in Bible Belt states in America, especially in Tennessee, where we live at the moment. Millions—saved and lost—see these scriptures as they drive down a highway. John 3:16 is sometimes quoted: "For God so loved the world, that he gave his only begotten Son, that whosoever believeth in him shall not perish, but have everlasting life" (KJV). If the Word and the Spirit were inseparable, then why do not all lost people get saved when they read this? The answer is, because the Spirit does not always *apply* the Word. Why not? Because God is sovereign.

In other words, there are times when God chooses to withhold His conscious presence. Isaiah discovered a truth we all face sooner or later: "Truly, you are a God who hides himself, O God of Israel, the Savior" (Isa. 45:15). That said, there will be those who foolishly choose *not* to take oil in their lamps as we all await the coming of the Bridegroom (Matt. 25:3). The lamp is a symbol of the Word: "Your word is a lamp to my feet and a light to my path" (Ps. 119:105). The oil is a symbol of the Holy Spirit. When Samuel poured the oil upon David, "the Spirit of the LORD rushed upon David from that day forward" (1 Sam. 16:13).

Jonathan Edwards (1703–1758) preached "Sinners in the Hands of an Angry God" on July 8, 1741, in Enfield, Connecticut. As great conviction seized his hearers, people were seen holding on to tree trunks to keep from sliding into Hell. But later on Edwards preached the same sermon in Northampton, Massachusetts, and there was no apparent effect whatever.

One would hope for unusual power every time one preaches. However, even the great apostle Paul was acutely aware that he might speak to people without the conscious enablement of the Spirit. This is why he prayed to be given *words*—utterance, unusual ability to think and preach when the Holy Spirit not only pours thoughts into one's mind but also grants boldness for which there is no natural explanation. Merely to preach doctrine, however accurate that teaching might be, would not be enough. My mentor, Dr. Lloyd-Jones, used to slap the wrists of those "sound" preachers who were "perfectly orthodox, perfectly useless."

In a word: we need not only the Scriptures but also

the power of God. It is the conscious power of God that (surely) every preacher wants.

HOW WELL DO YOU KNOW YOUR BIBLE?

And yet it is sadly true today that most Christians— whether liberal, Evangelical, or Charismatic—*do not know their Bibles*. It does not help that less and less expository preaching exists in the church today throughout the world. Topical or motivational preaching has largely dominated the airwaves in our day. Not that there is anything wrong with topical or motivational preaching. The best of God's servants have done it and still do. But a key component of expository preaching is a high view of Scripture. One is hardly motivated to preach chapter by chapter—not to mention verse by verse—if they do not believe the Holy Spirit inspires every word.

I will never forget preaching through the little Book of Jude. It has only twenty-five verses. I spent the better part of a year in Jude. When I came across a difficult verse in Jude, which happened more than once, it was my conviction of the infallibility of this little book that kept me mining for gold. And I found gold, I can tell you. When part of me wanted to give up—knowing few if any would notice—I still pressed on to get to the bottom of Jude's meaning. I am not saying that I or anyone else can ever get to the *bottom* of any part of the Word of God. But I am stating categorically that my best moments in Jude— and every book I preached at Westminster Chapel—came through careful, painful, determined, and prayerful waiting on the Holy Spirit to understand a particular book or verse. It paid off.

We live in the "me" generation. So many of us have catered to the "What's in it for me?" appetite of our generation. Hardly anyone asks, "What's in it for God?"

The Bible is the infallible Word of God. Referring to the Old Testament, Paul wrote:

> All Scripture is breathed out by God and profitable for teaching, for reproof, for correction, and for training in righteousness.
>
> —2 TIMOTHY 3:16

Peter wrote:

> For no prophecy was ever produced by the will of man, but men spoke from God as they were carried along by the Holy Spirit.
>
> —2 PETER 1:21

In addition to this, Peter affirmed the epistles of the apostle Paul as being Scripture:

> Our beloved brother Paul also wrote to you according to the wisdom given him, as he does in all his letters when he speaks in them of these matters. There are some things in them that are hard to understand, which the ignorant and unstable twist to their own destruction, as they do the other Scriptures.
>
> —2 PETER 3:15–16

God used *people* in writing the Bible, yes. Their personalities, style, cultural backgrounds, and theological presuppositions are apparent. But their words are still Spirit-breathed and infallible.

THE WORD OF GOD IN PREACHING, PRINT, PERSON

Peter said, "...whoever speaks, as one who speaks oracles of God" (1 Pet. 4:11). *Oracles* comes from *logia*—from *logos*, word. The New International Version translates it "the very words of God." The idea of oracle is that the Deity speaks through the person. Ideal preaching would be when God Himself owns our words so much that the hearers feel as if God Himself is confronting them.

Consider the preaching of Jesus: it was a case of being confronted by God Himself, for Jesus was (and is) God, and all His words mirrored the will of the Father (John 5:19). This is why His hearers were astonished; He spoke not as the scribes did but with authority (Matt. 7:28–29). Authority is what characterized Peter's preaching on the day of Pentecost, as I mentioned in my introduction. The scoffing that preceded Peter's sermon turned into people being "cut to the heart" and asking, "What shall we do?" (Acts 2:37).

DEFINITION OF PREACHING

That sermon embodies what preaching was meant to be: the proclamation of the Word of God *through human personality*. A person's background, culture, accent, natural ability, and education—or lack of it—will often be apparent, even if the person speaks with great anointing and power. During the Cane Ridge Revival (1801) in Bourbon County, Kentucky, called America's Second Great Awakening by church historians, many uneducated preachers joined in exhorting simultaneously with a half dozen others who were preaching at a large camp meeting. Hundreds and hundreds were converted. Mockers who showed up to criticize got saved. Because many of these preachers were uneducated but effective, many were led to believe that education and training were not only unnecessary but a hindrance to the Holy Spirit.

The landmark event had a lasting influence in the region. My church in Ashland, Kentucky, was possibly a part of the last vestige of the Cane Ridge phenomenon. I grew up hearing pastors and visiting evangelists who were mostly uneducated—that is, none that I know of had a college or university degree. But they knew their Bibles.

Agree or disagree, Spurgeon has been quoted as saying, "We cannot teach a person *how* to preach, but we can teach him *what* to preach." That said, the preacher can make mistakes. Huge mistakes. But what we have in Scripture is infallible, faithful, and absolutely true. God saw to that.

To put it another way, the Word of God in *print* and the Word of God in *person* have this in common: the divine and human factor. Jesus was God *as though* He were not man; He was man *as though* He were not God. "In the beginning was the Word, and the Word was with God, and the Word was God....And the Word became flesh" (John 1:1, 14). Likewise, the Scriptures are from God *as though* apart from those who wrote it, and yet those who wrote it showed their personalities *as though* they were on their own and given full liberty to express what they felt and believed. Therefore, the Word of God incarnate and the Word of God in print have this in common. As Jesus was without sin and His words were without error, so too the Scriptures are doctrinally and theologically inerrant.

When I first started preaching over sixty years ago, many people knew their Bibles. I could quote many scriptures from memory, but so too could many who listened. I often assumed that they knew what I was talking about without my having to explain what I meant. But not so today.

One of the greatest adjustments I have had to make—and am still having to make—is to *assume nothing* when I preach and when I write. I must keep in mind that many of my hearers and readers—thank God for the exceptions—will need my help to grow in their understanding and knowledge of Scripture.

It is a new generation, somewhat like the new pharaoh who did not know Joseph (Exod. 1:8). There was a time when all Egypt rejoiced in Joseph and his family, but that era did not last. There came a new pharaoh who owed Joseph nothing, a new generation who did not appreciate Joseph—indeed, a generation who felt threatened by Joseph's legacy.

It is much like that today. So many people in the church do not know their Bibles because they do not often read their Bibles. Not only that, church leaders themselves often do not know their Bibles; neither do they urgently encourage Bible reading. Worst of all, there is an ever-increasing number of people in the pulpit and pew who have not been persuaded by the inner testimony of the Holy Spirit that the Bible is the Word of God.

This is how we know that the Bible is the Word of God: by the inner testimony of the Holy Spirit. There are those who have tried to lean on the so-called "external" proofs of Scripture—archaeology, testimonies of people who say what the Bible has meant to them, and so on. These external proofs will not totally persuade. Only the Holy Spirit totally persuades. And because there has been a diminishing of the knowledge of the Holy Spirit in our day, it is not surprising that many people are "tossed to and fro" by "every wind of doctrine" (Eph. 4:14).

Many years ago, when I spent summers in Washington, DC, I became fairly well acquainted with an orthodox Jewish rabbi. He even invited me to his home for dinner. He corresponded with me when I was a student at Trevecca Nazarene University. I tried to convert him! But he was still gracious to me, and I learned from him. He was not only convinced that Moses wrote the first five books in the Old Testament, but that *God* wrote those five books as though Moses "had nothing to do with what he wrote." God dictated what Moses said. Those were the rabbi's words to me.

I am not saying that. I believe the men God chose to write the thirty-nine books of the Old Testament and the twenty-seven books of the New Testament had full liberty in what they said. It happens that what they believed and wrote was absolutely true. That does not mean that they could not make mistakes *when not* writing Scripture. They were fallible men. But when they wrote what became parts of the Bible, God overruled and they wrote what was and is true when it comes to doctrine.

What I write in this book (and all my books) is not Scripture. My writing as well my preaching is not Holy Scripture. During the writing process, I give my manuscripts to trusted friends. Some of them pick it to pieces, and then my editor makes corrections. I need all the help I can get! I know one writer (his editor told me) who will not let his editor change a single word—because he thinks God wrote his stuff!

I would never say that in a thousand years.

However, I would say of the apostle Paul that his *letters* are infallible. He himself wasn't. He was only a man. Luke tells of when Paul lost his temper (see Acts 23:3), something Jesus never did. Paul was capable of making mistakes. But when he wrote his epistles, God overruled, and we can embrace Paul's words wholeheartedly. So too with Matthew, Mark, Luke, and John, as well as the Old Testament and all the rest of the New Testament writers. You may safely read all of Scripture, knowing that the same faithful God who sent His Son into the world to die on a cross made sure His Son's words were recorded without error and the apostles chosen to write what we call the New Testament gave us infallible teaching.

God would not send His Son to us and then allow what He came to do be forgotten. That is why we have the Bible. God gave us our Bibles. Are you thankful for the Bible? Have you thought where we would be today without Bibles? If then God gave us Bibles, does He not want us to know what is in them?

Back in the 1950s and 1960s a phenomenon called neoorthodoxy emerged in Europe and spread to America. It became fashionable to say that the Bible "contains" the Word of God. Those who were proponents of this view would come short of saying that the Bible *is* the Word of God. Instead, they would say it "contains" the Word of God, leaving people to pick and choose the parts they surmise to be the authentic Word of God. The consequence was that people in ever-increasing numbers doubted the reliability of Holy Scripture. Many pastors became disillusioned and left the ministry entirely. Neoorthodoxy turned out to be a dangerous fad. I doubt any would go to the stake today for their neoorthodox views.

But I would go to the stake for what I believe.

I was in a graduate seminar at Southern Baptist Theological Seminary in 1971–1972. A fellow student in his final year said to me, "I don't know what I am going to do now. I came to this seminary believing in the Bible. I have been taught that it is a flawed document. I don't know what I will do in life from this point on." I am happy to say at this point that this same seminary has now embraced the infallibility of the Bible. That was not the case when I was there.

What held me in those days? Why did I not reject the Bible like others were doing? Answer: the inner testimony of the Holy Spirit kept me from giving in to teaching that is alien to Scripture. The Holy Spirit will do this for you too.

The degree to which we believe the Bible is infallible, reliable, and faithful often determines how much we care to read it. Mind you, the church being in a deep sleep has resulted even in many advanced Christians being dormant in their Bible reading. As I said, I can recall a day—in my lifetime—when *laymen* knew the Bible so well you could begin quoting a verse and many would finish it! In a previous generation not only did people read their Bibles, but they also memorized large portions of them. Such a practice has virtually perished from the earth today. I'm sorry, but even many preachers do not know their Bibles. Some only turn to the Scriptures when they need a sermon!

I would plead with every person who reads these lines to have a Bible reading plan, preferably one that will take you through the Bible in a year. It means reading approximately four chapters a day. Doing this (1) keeps you in the Word, and (2) gives you what the Holy Spirit will call to your remembrance later. One promise concerning the Holy Spirit is that He will call to remembrance what Jesus taught (John 14:26). Some say, "What I need is to be slain in the Spirit." I say: if you are empty-headed when you fall, you will be empty-headed when you get up. There will be nothing in your head of which the Holy Spirit can remind you!

WE NEED THE BIBLE PLUS THE HOLY SPIRIT

By now you understand that I am saying we need the Bible. However, I am also saying we need *more* than the Bible. We need the Holy Spirit. To quote Jack Taylor, there are those whose understanding of the Trinity is "God the Father, God the Son, and God the Holy Bible."[2] This candid observation is often accurate because of the presupposition that the Spirit and Word are inseparable. If the

17

Holy Spirit does not intervene and *apply* what I teach and write, my efforts are in vain. God must step in, or no one is gripped, no one is converted.

In a word: Scripture needs to be *applied*. This comes about by anointed preaching. But anointed preaching is never possible without the power of the Holy Spirit.

Chapter Two

BEING ON GOOD TERMS WITH THE HOLY SPIRIT

*Do not grieve the Holy Spirit of God, by whom
you were sealed for the day of redemption.*

—EPHESIANS 4:30

*Likewise the Spirit helps us in our weakness. For we
do not know what to pray for as we ought, but the
Spirit himself intercedes for us with groanings too
deep for words. And he who searches hearts knows
what is the mind of the Spirit, because the Spirit
intercedes for the saints according to the will of God.*

—ROMANS 8:26–27

I HAD A HEAD start in the matter of Christian living. My earliest memory of my father is seeing him on his knees for thirty minutes every morning before he went to work. He often read his Bible on his knees. He knew his Bible better than many preachers today and certainly prayed more than many preachers do today. It was the way he was brought up. He had a pastor who encouraged members of the church to spend thirty minutes a day in quiet time. He passed that heritage on to me and brought me up the same way. I am determined to pass this on as long as I have breath.

Martin Luther (1483–1546) endeavored to pray three hours every day. John Wesley (1703–1791) would not think of going into his daily work before he prayed two hours each day, usually rising at four o'clock in the morning. According to a recent poll, participated in by thousands of church leaders on both sides of the Atlantic, the average church leader today—minister, evangelist, pastor, bishop, vicar, rector—spends *four minutes a day* in personal quiet time. And you wonder why the church is asleep.

How much do you pray? How much do you read your Bible? How well do you know your Bible?

Would you like to be on good terms with the Holy Spirit? Then get to know what He wrote! He wrote the Bible. He is not ashamed of what He wrote. The Bible is the Holy Spirit's greatest product. You will have the Holy Spirit's anointing to the degree that you honor what the Holy Spirit *wrote*.

"My people are destroyed from lack of knowledge," said the prophet (Hos. 4:6). God wants all of us to be well acquainted with especially two things about Him: His Word and His ways. His Word refers to the Bible—the Old and New Testaments; His ways refer to His characteristics. "They have not known my *ways*," God lamented of His ancient people (Heb. 3:10, emphasis added). Moses, being assured that his ways pleased the Lord and that he could ask for anything, requested, "Show me now your ways" (Exod. 33:13).

God has *ways*. The Holy Spirit has *ways*. You may not like His ways. Moreover, He will not adjust to you; you must adjust to Him.

How does one get to know God's ways? How do you get to know anybody's way? Answer: by spending time with them. In my book *Did You Think to Pray?* (Charisma House) I put considerable emphasis on *time* spent with God. Children spell love T-I-M-E. That is what they want more than anything—time with their parents, time with those they look up to. We show how much we esteem a person by how much time we give to them.

My wife knows my *ways*. She knows how I think. She knows how I will react to a book, a sermon, a political speech, or new people I meet. I have a handful of friends who truly know my ways. They have spent considerable time with me.

Do not underestimate how well you get to know God's ways merely by spending time with Him.

I would urge every reader of this book to spend thirty minutes a day alone with God. You can count the Bible reading as part of that, but remember that time spent with God is never wasted. The following sentence is attributed to Martin Luther, although I cannot find it in his writings: "I have so much to do that if I didn't spend at least three hours a day in prayer, I would never get it all done."[1] Whether he said these words or not, we know Luther was a man of prayer. The idea being expressed is that the busier he got, the more essential prayer became. Most of us would excuse ourselves from praying more if we had a busy day.

The principle is this: give God His 10 percent and live on the 90 percent you keep for yourself. My dad used to say, "I sometimes think the 90 percent even goes further than the 100 percent!" Likewise, the more time you give to God, the more you get done! I am assuming you will use common sense when I suggest these things; don't try to pray around the clock! I promise you, give God thirty minutes a day—one hour or more if you are in full-time ministry—and you will get more done than you would have had you neglected quiet time with the Lord. Even Jesus needed this. "And rising very early in the morning, while it was still dark, he departed and went out to a desolate place, and there he prayed" (Mark 1:35).

The time of day is not as important as choosing a time when you can be most alert and effective. If you are not a morning person, pray in the evenings. Time alone with the Lord will bring you closer to Him and enable you to get to know His ways.

ONE OF THE HOLY SPIRIT'S WAYS

My most cherished insight at Westminster Chapel was to discover the sensitivity of the Holy Spirit. Arguably it is the most life-changing concept I have come across. I came

to grasp this before I faced the challenge of totally forgiving those who hurt me and betrayed me. It was my
awareness of the sensitivity of the Spirit that caused me to
realize the importance of total forgiveness. The sensitivity
of the Spirit and total forgiveness are reciprocal; they are
truly inseparable. You grieve the Spirit when you don't forgive; when you totally forgive, the Holy Spirit will move
into your heart with unfathomable peace and joy.

One essential feature of the Holy Spirit's ways is that
He is—like it or not—a very, very sensitive person. The
third member of the Trinity is a person, and one of His
ways is that He gets His feelings hurt—easily. You may say,
"He should not be like that." But that is the way He is. Get
over it, or you will never get to know Him. He will not
adjust to you; you must adjust to Him.

Years ago a British couple was sent by their denomination to be missionaries in Israel. After a few weeks in
their new home near Jerusalem they noticed that a dove
had come to live in the eaves of their house. They also
noticed that whenever they would slam a door, the dove
would fly away. Every time they got into an argument with
each other, the dove would fly away. One day Sandy said to
Bernice, "Have you noticed the dove?"

"Oh yes," she replied. "It is like a seal of God on our
being in Israel."

Sandy noted how the dove would fly away every time
they slammed a door shut or got into a heated argument.
"I'm so afraid the dove will fly away and never come back,"
Bernice said.

Then Sandy looked at her and said, "Either the dove

adjusts to us, or we adjust to the dove." They changed their lives—just to keep the dove around.

The New Testament depicts the Holy Spirit as a dove, and yet not only a dove; sometimes wind, sometimes fire. But why a dove? The dove is a timid bird. Doves and pigeons are in the same family. Anatomically they are identical, but temperamentally they are vastly different.

In my book *Pigeon Religion* (Charisma House) I show nineteen differences between doves and pigeons. I won't go into these now, but I will mention two things. First, a pigeon is boisterous, noisy, and unafraid of people. Doves are gentle, loving, and afraid of people. You cannot get physically close to a dove; it will fly away before you can touch it.

Like a dove, the Holy Spirit is easily grieved and quenched. Like it or not, *the easiest thing in the world to do is to grieve the Holy Spirit.* You may need time to absorb the previous sentence, but believe me, it is not an exaggeration.

Second, you can train a pigeon, but you cannot train a dove. With pigeon religion, you tell the Holy Spirit what to do. But with the authentic Holy Spirit, He tells you what to do. The reason I wrote *Pigeon Religion* was to show how many people don't know the difference between the authentic Holy Spirit and the counterfeit, just as many people don't know the difference between a dove and a pigeon. I've heard people say, "The Holy Ghost came down in our church Sunday." But when I got to the bottom of it, I was given pause—it was pigeon religion.

The bottom line is: the Holy Spirit is indeed a very sensitive person. When Paul said, "Do not *grieve* the Holy

Spirit" (Eph. 4:30, emphasis added), he used a Greek word that means to get your feelings hurt. The Holy Spirit, as I said, gets His feelings hurt very, very easily.

The greatest challenge I have *ever* faced is to try to go a day or two without grieving the Spirit. You do it when you do not mean to; you do it when you try not to! You may say, "That's not fair." I understand because I have thought that a thousand times. But that is one of the *ways* of the Holy Spirit.

I have come to understand this aspect of the Holy Spirit by spending more and more time with Him. The more I get to know Him, the more I see how sinful I am—so frail, weak, pitiful, and unworthy. I have also discovered that you rarely know it at the time when you grieve the Spirit. You feel nothing when you make the unguarded comment to a friend or stranger; show your frustration with the old woman at the cash register in a supermarket who has all day and you are in a hurry; speak impatiently on the phone with an airline representative who is terse; honk your horn at the slow car in front of you; or say an unkind word about someone. "I told the truth," you may say. Granted, but you still grieved the Holy Spirit; the dove flies away for the moment.

The more time we spend with God, the more we see His holiness and our sin. It is not that the Holy Spirit ever deserts us when we stumble; no, He never leaves us (John 14:15–16). But we lose the *sense* of His presence: clear thinking, insight into a difficult verse in the Bible, knowing what grieves the Spirit.

God is gracious and forgiving. But He wants us to know

His ways. Getting to know His ways means spending time with Him. There may be shortcuts, but I have not found them.

During my final year in London, I was asked to address one hundred ministers that had convened at Holy Trinity Brompton. They gave me ten minutes to speak on the subject of prayer. I used those ten minutes to urge every one of those ministers—mostly pastors and vicars—to spend at least *one hour a day* in quiet time. I should tell you that my talk was deeply appreciated. We all need to be reminded of the most elementary and obvious things such as time alone with God.

When you and I stand before the judgment seat of Christ (which we all will do), we may regret how we spent our time and money while on this earth. But we will have no regrets regarding how much *time* we spent alone with the Lord or how much *money* we gave to Him. We will almost certainly regret we didn't spend more time with Him. I hope this book will be used of the Holy Spirit to impel all who read these lines to begin *now* spending more time alone with God. Nothing is more heartwarming than knowing God likes our company!

Chapter Three

How to Get More of the Holy Spirit

But earnestly desire the higher gifts.

—1 Corinthians 12:31

_Be filled with the Spirit, addressing one another
in psalms and hymns and spiritual songs, singing
and making melody to the Lord with your heart,
giving thanks always and for everything to God
the Father in the name of our Lord Jesus Christ._

—Ephesians 5:18–20

WOULD YOU LIKE more of the Holy Spirit? I certainly would.

Some people might object to the idea of "more" of the Holy Spirit. They take the view that you either have all there is of the Holy Spirit, or you don't. That is a superficial observation—and very misleading indeed. The thrust of all the New Testament letters is about increasing our faith, getting closer to God, and getting more of Him. Only Jesus had the Holy Spirit without limit (John 3:34). You and I have but a "measure" of the Spirit, which is why we have a measure of faith (Rom. 12:3).

The disciples asked of Jesus, "Increase our faith" (Luke 17:5). As one put it, "I believe; help my unbelief" (Mark 9:24). You and I are often in this very position; we struggle but want God to increase our faith. This comes in proportion to getting a greater measure of the Holy Spirit.

I wrote this book for *every* Christian. Part of it might seem directed to preachers or leaders, but *all* Christians— men and women, young and old—need it. If you are not a pastor or leader, this part of the book still applies to you— whatever your job, gift, or calling may be. It might also help you gain an appreciation for the responsibility your pastor and church leaders carry and cause you to pray harder for them. All readers will benefit from what follows.

Do not take what I say in these lines as being from an expert. I said at the beginning that I did not see the Holy Spirit work in my ministry as I hoped—and still pray for. What follows are suggestions. They have led me to the little bit of anointing I have. God has not finished with me yet. But here is what I put to you.

SEVEN WAYS TO RECEIVE
MORE OF THE HOLY SPIRIT

1. Ask for it.

As I mentioned earlier, Paul requested that the Ephesians pray for him to be given "words" when he spoke. Jesus said that we should ask and the Father will give the Holy Spirit to us:

> And I tell you, ask, and it will be given to you; seek, and you will find; knock, and it will be opened to you. For everyone who asks receives, and the one who seeks finds, and to the one who knocks it will be opened. What father among you, if his son asks for a fish, will instead of a fish give him a serpent; or if he asks for an egg, will give him scorpion? If you then, who are evil, know how to give good gifts to your children, how much more will the heavenly Father give the Holy Spirit to those who ask him!
>
> —LUKE 11:9–13

James said:

> You do not have, because you do not ask.
>
> —JAMES 4:2

Readers of my book *Holy Fire* might recall my life-changing experience of the Holy Spirit when driving from Palmer, Tennessee, to Nashville on October 31, 1955. What happened came as a result of my *asking* for more of God. To my amazement—I have never gotten over it—I suddenly witnessed Jesus interceding for me at the right hand of God the Father. After being in the Spirit for an hour, I literally heard these words of Jesus to the Father: "He wants it." The Father replied, "He can have it." Immediately a warm surge of the Spirit entered my heart. A peace I did not know was possible in this life was given to me. It changed my life and also my theology. I have never been the same since.

And yet I have asked many times for over sixty years, what was the *it* that Jesus and the Father referred to? I have come up with several possible answers: *It* could have meant the baptism of the Holy Spirit, the sealing of the Spirit, the rest of faith (Heb. 4:1, 10), rest for the soul (Matt. 11:29), what Charles Wesley (1707–1788) called "promised rest" in his hymn "Love Divine, All Loves Excelling,"[1] or "joy unspeakable" (1 Pet. 1:8, KJV). I could add to this list. In any case, *it* would mean *more of the Holy Spirit.* I was praying that day for more of the Holy Spirit. I was literally pleading with the Lord.

If you want more of the Holy Spirit, *ask* for more of Him.

> O what peace we often forfeit,
> O what needless pain we bear,
> All because we do not carry
> Everything to God in prayer![2]
> —JOSEPH M. SCRIVEN (1819–1886)

Did you think to ask? Did you think to pray?

2. Spend time pleading with God and waiting for Him to act.

This is often where the rubber hits the road. Speaking directly to pastors and leaders for a moment, one must never count sermon preparation time as quiet time. Preparing a sermon is your job! Yes, you can certainly pray as you prepare. But if you count sermon preparation time as your time alone with God, you are cheating.

I ask all my hearers and readers to spend at least thirty minutes a day alone with God—and they have to go to work. Therefore, I do not count my preparation of a sermon as time with God; I see sermon preparation or book writing as my job. I must get to know God and His ways by spending time with Him *before I begin to work on a sermon or write a book.*

You might ask: "But how can I know God's ways merely by spending time with Him?" The answer is, *because you do*! Time alone with God honors Him, affirms His Word and His promise. When you do this, part of the reward is beginning to know His ways. You reap this benefit merely by consciously spending time with Him, boring though it might seem at the time.

It is wonderful to know God's ways. This means you are coming to know God in a way that ancient Israel didn't! God lamented, "They have not known my ways" (Heb. 3:10). But God will not say this of *you* when you take time to spend time with Him.

The power comes not from how much I know, how much I read commentaries and books, or how much time I spend in fellowship with godly friends. It comes from seeking God's face in the equivalent of a "tent of meeting."

> Now Moses used to take the tent and pitch it outside the camp, far off from the camp, and he called it the tent of meeting. And everyone who sought the LORD would go out to the tent of

> meeting, which was outside the camp....When
> Moses entered the tent, the pillar of cloud would
> descend and stand at the entrance of the tent, and
> the LORD would speak with Moses....Thus the
> LORD used to speak to Moses face to face, as a
> man speaks to his friend.
>
> —EXODUS 33:7, 9, 11

Intimacy with God comes by making an effort and spending as much time with Him as you can. Never forget that He is a jealous God (Exod. 20:5). If you do not like this aspect of God's nature, I'm sorry, but that is simply the way He is. God wants you to love Him for being *just like He is.*

I can make this promise to you: get to know Him by spending time with Him, and you will find yourself overwhelmed with amazement that we have a God like Him.

This chapter is about getting on good terms with the Holy Spirit. If this is what you and I truly want, we will not be able to take shortcuts. It takes time, but the effort is worth it!

3. Know your Bible backward and forward.

You almost certainly should begin with a Bible reading plan. Any will do, but it should be one that takes you through the Bible in a year. My Robert Murray M'Cheyne (1813–1843) Bible reading plan takes me through the Psalms and the New Testament twice a year. (I'll explain more about M'Cheyne in chapter 7.)

Those in the ministry should read the Bible not merely with a view of getting a sermon—or even a "rhema word." Read it for its own sake. Get to know it. Know the patriarchs—Abraham, Isaac, Jacob, and Joseph. Know the history of Israel. Get to understand God's dealings with Moses. Learn the place of the Law in God's scheme of redemption. Know the Psalms and the Prophets. Understand the teachings of Jesus. Be acquainted with the miracles and how the Holy Spirit came down on the day of Pentecost. See and grasp the history of the early church in the Book of Acts. Fall in love with the writings of Paul and all the apostles. You are reading God's own Word.

There is no knowledge under the sun that is equal to a vast knowledge of Holy Scripture. I would not trade my knowledge of the Bible for any amount of money or with the most learned physicist, philosopher, or physician in this world. What I have, you can have. Anybody can have this. It is obtained by simply reading the Bible so much that you get to know it—all over.

I will make a second promise to you: *you will never be sorry you spent time with God's Word.* Whether you are a minister or a cab driver, a children's pastor or a server in a restaurant, a worship leader or an accountant—I could go on and on—get to know your Bible better than any other book. The reward is incalculable. Being on good terms with the Holy Spirit is greater than being connected to celebrities, royalty, or the president. Never forget what the great evangelist Dwight L. Moody (1837–1899) said: "The Bible was not given to increase our knowledge, but to change lives."[3]

4. Live a holy life.

One might think this goes without saying, but I believe it has to be said. None of us are naturally prone to *want* holiness. Holiness and sanctification (the process by which we become more and more holy) may be used interchangeably. We are all congenitally allergic to holiness! If the robust desire for holiness were automatic with faith in Christ, we would not *need* the epistles of the New Testament. The reason we have the epistles is that seeking after holiness—sanctification—must be *taught*.

The New Testament doctrine of sanctification is the doctrine of gratitude. It is our way of saying, "Thank You, Lord, for saving my soul." Gratitude is sometimes spontaneous, but often it is not. Jesus healed ten lepers, but *only one* came back to say thank you. Jesus' immediate observation: "Where are the nine?" (Luke 17:17). This tells me three things:

1. God loves gratitude. He is honored when we take time to thank Him.

2. God hates ingratitude. He puts it alongside the most heinous sins (Rom. 1:21–32; 2 Tim. 3:2).

3. Gratitude must be taught.

We need to be taught and reminded to be grateful, just as Paul reminded his followers:

- "Give thanks in all circumstances" (1 Thess. 5:18).

- "By prayer and supplication with thanksgiving let your requests be made known to God" (Phil. 4:6).

- "Continue steadfastly in prayer, being watchful in it with thanksgiving" (Col. 4:2).

Likewise, holiness must be taught:

- "For this is the will of God, your sanctification" (1 Thess. 4:3).

- "...that those who have believed in God may be careful to devote themselves to good works" (Titus 3:8).

- "Strive...for the holiness without which no one will see the Lord" (Heb. 12:14).

- "You shall be holy, for I am holy" (1 Pet. 1:16; Lev. 11:44).

In a word: if you want to be on good terms with the Spirit of God, remember that He is the *Holy* Spirit and that He wrote the Old and New Testaments. The epistles of the New Testament could be summed up as showing the necessity of holiness and how to live the holy life.

5. Witness to people—even strangers—on a one-to-one basis.

I hope what I now share with you will make you smile. It happens that I wrote the sentence in boldface preceding this paragraph while on a flight from Chicago to Seattle. Next to me was an orthopedic surgeon from Chicago. My wife, Louise, was suffering from acute pain from a herniated disc. She had an operation on her back seven years before. The odds of sitting next to a surgeon who performs virtually the same operation was very remote. I learned a lot from him and discovered he was Jewish. I returned to writing this book and began this paragraph. This thought suddenly interrupted me: "Either I believe what I am writing—or I don't. If I don't practice what I preach in this very book and start talking to this man about Jesus, I am a hypocrite."

I prayed for wisdom, and then turned to him and changed the subject to Jesus Christ. Having told him that I am a Christian minister, I asked, "Do you have any patients that talk to you about Jesus Christ?"

"No," he replied. I told him I had written a book with an orthodox Jewish rabbi (*The Christian and the Pharisee*, FaithWords). I then asked, "Do you know for sure that if you were to die today, you would go to Heaven?"

"No."

I then asked, "If you were to stand before God—and you will—and He were to ask you—and He might—'Why should I let you into My Heaven?' what would you say?" He wasn't sure what to say, only that he thought he had been a good person. I then presented the Gospel to him, that Jesus of Nazareth was His Messiah who died on a cross for our sins. He wasn't particularly interested in what I had to say, but I said to him, "If someone else talks to you like this in the near future, it will show you that God is on your case." He smiled. He also thanked me when I asked to pray for him. I will probably never see him again.

Why should one witness to people like this? Answer: First, because we are commanded to do this by Jesus Himself (Matt. 28:19; Mark 16:15). Second, because the early church—even apart from the apostles—went about doing this (Acts 8:1–4). Third, sharing the faith results in deepening our understanding of what we have in Christ (Philem. 6, NIV).

Years ago a British lawyer came into my vestry at Westminster Chapel to say, "I believe I am called to preach." I suggested that he test this call by joining us in witnessing to lost people in the streets of Westminster on Saturday morning. He immediately replied, "I am no good at witnessing to one person, but I am good at speaking to thousands." I replied to him as gently as I could, "If you are not willing to witness to one person, you are not called to witness from a pulpit to thousands." He never came back again.

Within a few weeks of becoming the minister of Westminster Chapel, I asked the congregation, "How many of you out there have *never* led a soul to Jesus Christ?" I was speaking to our regular church members when I asked this. But I could equally address those in the ministry with the same question! A minister who cannot witness to a person on a one-to-one basis is—in my honest opinion— not fit to be preaching the Gospel from the pulpit.

We are all called to do this. If we see the lost start coming to Christ by the millions, I believe it will happen because the sleeping giant called the body of Christ wakes up, gets fired up, and starts talking about Jesus Christ to their neighbors, friends, and everyone they meet.

If you've read my other books, it is likely you've read the story about the time I invited Arthur Blessitt, the man who has carried a wooden cross all over the world (and currently holds the world record for longest ongoing pilgrimage[4]), to preach for six weeks in a row at Westminster Chapel in the spring of 1982. He preached on "the heartbeat of God," which he believed was to bring the lost to the saving knowledge of Jesus Christ. Arthur talked about witnessing to all people wherever they were.

One of our deacons who had been a great supporter of my ministry was incensed over Arthur's blatant preaching. He vowed never to return until Arthur was gone. Then when Arthur was gone, this deacon recruited several other deacons to oust me as the minister. They almost succeeded. But incredibly the whole crisis started with Arthur's intentional emphasis on all people being witnesses wherever they are!

Are you a witness for Jesus? Do you talk to your friends? Have you ever led a soul to Christ?

A person once asked Arthur Blessitt, "Why does God seem to talk to you directly, but He doesn't talk to me like that?"

Arthur replied by asking, "Have you ever had an impulse to witness to someone you didn't know?"

The person replied, "As a matter of fact, I have."

Arthur said to this person, "Then start obeying that impulse, and the voice of the Lord will become clearer and clearer."

There is nothing like witnessing for Jesus Christ to bring about intimacy with God—that is, if intimacy with the Holy Spirit is what you want.

It is my view that the church today is asleep. That was Jesus' assessment of the church in the very last days—asleep. Having described the last days in Matthew 24, Jesus said in Matthew 25:1, "Then"—at that time, during the very last days—"the kingdom of heaven will be like ten virgins." Five were wise, and five were foolish, but they *all* slumbered and slept (v. 5). Yes, that is the best way I know to describe the church today—asleep. As I wrote in my book *Prepare Your Heart for the Midnight Cry* (Charisma House), in the natural world you don't know you were asleep until you wake up. The same truth applies in the spiritual world. We—the body of Christ, the church—don't know we are asleep spiritually. We will not realize we have been sleeping until we wake up.

When the midnight cry described in Matthew 25 occurs, we will awaken and unashamedly witness for Jesus Christ to everyone—friends, neighbors, and strangers. Unfortunately, for now, a spirit of fear virtually paralyzes the church and keeps us in spiritual slumber.

My point is: if it is power you want, try talking to people about Jesus wherever you go.

6. Seek honor and praise from God, not people.

John 5:44 has been my life verse for over sixty years. I am not sure why it has remained with me lifelong, but I know it first gripped me back in 1956 because two of my mentors often quoted it. When I say "life verse," I don't mean to suggest for one minute that I have lived up to this verse. I have failed many times, but I have sought to live by it.

John 5:44 shows that we should live and speak before an audience of one—namely God alone. Malachi 3:16 says that God eavesdrops on our conversations. If we start speaking to one another with the awareness that God

Himself is listening, it might drastically change the tenor of our conversations.

John 5:44 reveals the reason the Jews missed their Messiah: they were addicted to the approval of fellow Jews. They did not want to lose a friend by admitting that Jesus of Nazareth was the Messiah of God. Had they been motivated by the honor that comes from the only God—as they should have been—they would not have been motivated by fear of one another but by the fear of God. This goes to show that you and I could miss what God is doing today if we are more worried about what people think than what God thinks. Be motivated by the honor and praise that comes from God alone!

7. Esteem the *fruit* of the Spirit as much as the *gifts* of the Spirit and vice versa.

It has been my observation that Spirit people tend to emphasize the gifts of the Spirit. Some feel the gifts are decidedly more important; we should talk about the gifts—often speaking in tongues. I'm sorry, but I run into a lot of Charismatic Christians that only want to talk about speaking in tongues and praying in tongues. They sometimes give the impression that they are a cut above those who don't speak in tongues. Some of them also tend to take the fruit of the Spirit for granted.

Word people seem to emphasize the fruit of the Spirit. They tend to go quiet when it comes to the gifts. It seems to make some of them nervous!

In my book *In Pursuit of His Glory* (Charisma House) I tell how I first began speaking in tongues. A rather close relative said of it to Louise, "I enjoyed R. T.'s latest book, but did he have to mention tongues?"

For many Word people, speaking in tongues is about the most offensive thing on the planet! With some denominations, for example, you can commit adultery, be divorced several times, and be a Freemason, and you will be forgiven. But if the word leaks out that you speak in tongues, you are immediately kept at a distance, held in suspicion, and kept at bay indefinitely! I wish it were not true. And yet we must be willing to accept the stigma that comes with being unashamed of the gift of speaking or praying in tongues. I don't mean to be unfair, but speaking personally, it is part of the price to pay if we want a greater anointing of the Spirit. Being kept at bay—or even rejected—is worth the price for a greater anointing. Would you not want a greater anointing than anything in the world?

Chapter Four

THE FRUIT OF THE SPIRIT

The fruit of the Spirit is love, joy, peace, patience, kindness, goodness, faithfulness, gentleness, self-control; against such things there is no law.

—GALATIANS 5:22–23

THE FRUIT—*NOT fruits*—of the Spirit springs from obedience. The fruit of the Spirit is a requirement of all believers. Whereas the gifts of the Spirit, to be explored in the next chapter, are sovereignly bestowed (1 Cor. 12:11, 18) and are irrevocable (Rom. 11:29), the fruit of the Spirit is what you and I are obliged to pursue.

The fruit of the Holy Spirit is the effect, or result, of living the Christian life in obedience. It is what *flows* in those who resist the "works of the flesh," namely, "sexual immorality, impurity, sensuality, idolatry, sorcery, enmity, strife, jealousy, fits of anger, rivalries, dissensions, divisions, envy, drunkenness, orgies" (Gal. 5:19–21). Those who give in to the works of the flesh forfeit their inheritance in the kingdom of God (v. 21).

To put it another way, the genuinely saved person has no choice; the fruit of the Spirit is a command. However, the gifts of the Spirit, while not commanded, should be sought after. As Paul put it, "earnestly desire the higher gifts" (1 Cor. 12:31). The fruit of the Spirit is a sign of obedience; the gifts, a sign of God's calling on your life.

Love

Love is listed first. Why? Possibly because showing *agape* love will likely incorporate all the other qualities on Paul's list. Three Greek words are translated as love: (1) *agape* is unselfish, self-giving love; (2) *eros* is physical love; and (3) *philia* is brotherly love. Galatians 5:22 uses *agape* love. If you truly experience this love, you will have joy, peace, patience, kindness, goodness, faithfulness, gentleness, and self-control. We find the proof in 1 Corinthians 13, where Paul unpacks the meaning of *agape* love. Once you grasp 1 Corinthians 13, you will discover that everything Paul calls the "fruit of the Spirit" is beautifully woven into 1 Corinthians 13. I have written an exposition of 1 Corinthians 13 in my book *Just Love* (Christian Focus Publications).

These things said, I must also state the two ways the fruit of the Spirit manifests:

1. Spontaneously

Strange as it may seem, sometimes love just erupts! Like a geyser that shoots out water without provocation or cause, love sometimes flows with no effort on our part. It comes easily. The Holy Spirit does this.

2. By an act of the will

On the other hand, the same person who experienced this love spontaneously yesterday struggles today. What do you do? You intentionally force yourself to keep no record of wrongs; you refuse to point the finger. You work at it. But *because* you have the Holy Spirit, *you can do it*. Yesterday it was easy. Today it is not easy.

Why? I believe that sometimes the Holy Spirit is simply waiting for *us* to make an effort. Either way, the result is to demonstrate to others that you truly show the fruit of the Spirit.

The kind of love listed in the fruit of the Spirit is a self-sacrificing, unselfish love. It is the love that lies behind God sending His Son into the world (John 3:16). It is perhaps best summed up in 1 Corinthians 13:5: love "keeps no record of wrongs" (NIV). Why do we keep records? To prove we have paid our bills. Why keep a record of wrongs? To bring up the past; to point the finger; to make a person feel guilty. When you experience *agape* love, you do not bring up one's guilty past. Just as God forgives, you forgive. It is the first fruit Paul mentions. The other qualities follow love, according to Paul.

There are also occasions when the fruit-of-the-Spirit love is manifested apart from the act of forgiveness. There are times when the dove comes down on us spontaneously without our consciously having to forgive by an act of the will. God may choose to show up when we are not even praying! He is both sovereign and gracious. The love that flows from the Spirit can even be experienced by refusing to give in to *any* temptation of the flesh—including sexual temptation, greed, or jealousy. The same fruit of the Spirit will often manifest through our dignifying a trial. In other words, instead of complaining and grumbling when a trial suddenly comes, we submit to it—as it "falleth from above," as the hymn "Like a River Glorious," quoted later, puts it.

The same can be said for other fruit of the Spirit. Whereas consciously forgiving others will result in love, joy, and peace, we may nonetheless discover such fruit of the Spirit because our lives are being directed by a sovereign, gracious God.

Joy

Joy is an internal feeling of great pleasure. The difference between joy and happiness is that joy is internal; happiness comes from external things that make us feel good—a kind letter, a raise in pay, a compliment. Joy, however, is internal. This pleasure flows from voluntarily refusing to point the finger at someone else. It is an act of the will.

When I refuse to point the finger—difficult though it

may sometimes be—the result is sooner or later the same: joy. Internal pleasure. I feel good that I resisted pointing the finger. It is as though the Spirit rewards me for keeping no record of wrongs. But, as I said before, one may experience joy by refusing to complain or not giving in to any temptations of the flesh.

Like love, joy can either come by an act of the will (as I've just described) or spontaneously. What I experienced years ago when driving in my car from Palmer to Nashville was spontaneous joy. It is quite impossible to describe. It was truly "joy unspeakable and full of glory" (1 Pet. 1:8, KJV). It lasted a good while, but one day—suddenly—it ended. After that I had to get my joy from voluntarily, actively, and intentionally overlooking faults in others that bother me. Or refusing to grumble. Or not speaking evil of another person—even if what I might have said was true! One can state what may well be true about another, but we will grieve the Spirit if our motive is to make another look bad.

Now you understand what I meant when I said that the fruit of the Spirit is sometimes spontaneous and sometimes by an act of the will. However, as I said, it is because you *have* the Holy Spirit that you can produce the same fruit by an act of your will.

Peace

This internal fruit of the Spirit is equally difficult to describe. It is not merely the absence of anxiety; it is the undeniable presence of a calm feeling deep inside. Calm is perhaps the best word to describe it. It is a feeling of self-control—a fruit that Paul includes at the end of the list. This old hymn describes it amazingly:

> Like a river glorious is God's perfect peace,
> Over all victorious, in its bright increase;
> Perfect, yet it floweth fuller every day,
> Perfect, yet it groweth deeper all the way.
>
> Stayed upon Jehovah, hearts are fully blest;
> Finding, as He promised, perfect peace and rest.
>
> Hidden in the hollow of His blessed hand,
> Never foe can follow, never traitor stand;
> Not a surge of worry, nor a shade of care,
> Not a blast of hurry touch the spirit there.
>
> Every joy or trial falleth from above,
> Traced upon our dial by the Sun of Love;
> We may trust Him fully, all for us to do;
> They who trust Him wholly find Him wholly true.[1]
> —FRANCES R. HAVERGAL (1836–1879)

You cannot turn on instant peace by an act of the will, but you can do what leads to it by intentionally overlooking another's faults, refusing to point the finger and telling God alone—not others—what you feel (Ps. 142:2).

Patience

Patience is the steadfastness to endure pain, delay, or trouble without getting angry or upset. Again, sometimes this is given with spontaneous ease; other times you force yourself not to complain. This is why James said we should *count* it—impute to the trial—pure joy when we fall into various kinds of trouble (Jas. 1:2). James added, "And let steadfastness have its full effect, that you may be perfect and complete, lacking in nothing" (v. 4).

Peter has his own list of qualities, similar to Paul's but not in the same order.

> For this very reason, make every effort to supplement your faith with virtue, and virtue with knowledge, and knowledge with self-control, and self-control with steadfastness, and steadfastness with godliness, and godliness with brotherly affection, and brotherly affection with love. For if these qualities are yours and are increasing, they keep you from being ineffective or unfruitful in the knowledge of our Lord Jesus Christ.
> —2 PETER 1:5–8

This passage shows that the order of the listed virtues is not of supreme importance; it shows how the minds of two godly men work differently. Also, whereas Paul lists some of these qualities as "fruit" of the Spirit, Peter puts the onus on us as if we are responsible for such a pursuit. The point is, the fruit of the Spirit listed by Paul and the qualities listed by Peter are what you and I are commanded to display.

As I mentioned, there is a difference between the *fruit* of the Spirit and the *gifts* of the Spirit. You and I are *required* to manifest love, patience, and brotherly affection; we are not required to have the gift of miracles or discerning of spirits, as we will see in the next chapter.

The writer of Hebrews wrote to discouraged Jewish believers, "You have need of endurance" (Heb. 10:36). Don't we all? Sometimes such a virtue flows passively without effort; other times, as I have been saying, we must make an effort to do these things because we do have the Holy Spirit.

Kindness

Paul said, "Love is patient and kind" (1 Cor. 13:4). Kindness means being considerate, friendly, or nice. Many years ago the Roman Catholic Church in America laid down three rules for winning converts:

1. Be kind.

2. Be kind.

3. Be kind.

I have learned that kindness goes very far in winning people over to your position. In the days I met with Yasser Arafat (1929–2004) and some Palestinians, I learned one thing for sure: our *doctrine* will not win them; showing that we care will win them. That's it. When they *feel* this from us, they are far more apt to listen to what we have to say.

This is why James makes a huge point, namely, that the "poor man" (Jas. 2:6) will not be impressed by our sound teaching but by our showing good works. James asked, "Can that faith save him [meaning the poor man]?" (v. 14). Answer: no, but our kindness is more likely to win him over.

Kindness, then, is a fruit of the Holy Spirit—even if you have to remind yourself to be kind!

Goodness

Goodness means, simply, being good, being decent, showing unselfishness. It's when we make an effort to do something helpful. We often use the expression, "That is good of you to do." It is the opposite of being bad, wicked, or immoral.

Luke says of Barnabas that he was "a good man" (Acts 11:24). For a human being to be called "a good man" in Holy Writ, you may safely mark it down that Barnabas was unusual. Those who knew Barnabas held him with such respect that when all were keenly suspicious of Saul of Tarsus—even after Saul's conversion—Barnabas was able to cause others to accept him (Acts 9:27). The disciples were first called Christians in Antioch when Barnabas was around (Acts 11:26).

When I first went to Trevecca Nazarene University in Nashville in 1953, I remember going to a store to buy something. I realized I forgot to bring money. The manager of the store said, "Did you say you were from Trevecca?" I responded in the affirmative. "Then you have good credit here. We all know those people are good." What a reputation!

Faithfulness

"A faithful man, who can find?" (Prov. 20:6, KJV). I quoted that verse in my very first sermon preached on December 2, 1954, in Nashville. My subject was "The Faithfulness of God," the text being "great is thy faithfulness" (Lam. 3:23, KJV).

Faithfulness means being trustworthy, being loyal, having integrity. A husband who is faithful is one who avoids sexual activity with another woman. Yes, a faithful man, who can find? Take loyalty, for example. I have come to the conclusion that there is no way one can know in advance whether a person will be loyal. I know of no test one can take, no question put in an interview that will help you determine whether a person will be faithful. A leader needs an assistant who will be loyal; a wife needs a husband who will be faithful; a person who is wealthy needs a person around him or her not only with wisdom but who will be trustworthy.

In any case, the fruit of the Spirit results in a person having the rare quality of integrity. Think about this for a moment. A person who follows the Holy Spirit will not cheat, lie, or betray. Yet, sadly, many church leaders today are discovered to be lacking in financial integrity or sexual faithfulness. Whatever else this indicates, it shows that such a person lacks the fruit of the Holy Spirit. If all Christians consistently obeyed the Lord by showing the fruit of the Spirit, there would be no unfaithfulness, sexual immorality, disloyalty, or mistrust in the church!

Gentleness

Gentleness comes from a Greek word meaning mild and sometimes translated as "meekness."[2] The funny thing is, in the Greco-Roman world this was no quality to be admired! Quite the opposite; the Greeks saw this as being cowardly and weak.

The Christian faith, however, has taken over this word to make it something not only to be admired but sought after. Jesus said, "Blessed are the meek" (Matt. 5:5). Meekness means that you won't be defensive if someone speaks against you. You will take criticism lying down. You will turn the other cheek.

Gentleness, then, means being mild-mannered or tender.

Love is "not easily provoked" (1 Cor. 13:5, KJV), not "irritable" (ESV). Jesus said of Himself, "I am gentle and lowly in heart" (Matt. 11:29). Moses was "very meek, more than all the people who were on the face of the earth" (Num. 12:3).

Meekness is not a quality the ancient Greeks admired. In today's world it is certainly not the way you win elections if in politics! However, it is a fruit of the Holy Spirit, and if you and I follow the Spirit with all our hearts, we will display this fruit of gentleness.

Self-control

Self-control comes from the Greek word *egkrateia*. It denotes "the virtue of one who masters his desires and passions, especially his sensual appetites."[3] It was reckoned to be a cardinal virtue by Socrates (c. 470–399 BC). For Philo (c. 20–50) it meant superiority to every desire. It was expressed in restraint, relating to food, sex, and use of the tongue. Paul used it regarding an athlete: "Every athlete exercises self-control in all things" (1 Cor. 9:25).

The fact that it is a fruit of the Holy Spirit is challenging for most of us. We all need self-control—whether regarding diet, exercise, watching television, or taking time off when we are working too hard. Because we have the Holy Spirit, says Paul, we *can* control how much we eat and whether we exercise, resist temptation, or give in to pleasure. It is surprising that we don't see this word more often. It is not in the four Gospels. It is also remarkable that Paul lists this fruit at the bottom of his list! He might have put it first!

The King James Version wrongly translates the Greek as "temperance," which brings to mind the old movement against legalizing alcohol in the United States. Don't let that mislead you into thinking this is about avoiding alcohol. The fruit of the Spirit will enable us to resist over-doing *anything*—whatever habit or temptation—that militates against godliness.

Having said all the above, how do you feel? Do you manifest the fruit of the Spirit? Read Galatians 5:22–23 again:

> The fruit of the Spirit is love, joy, peace, patience, kindness, goodness, faithfulness, gentleness, self-control.

We are not responsible for having the gifts of the Spirit, but—like it or not—we are responsible for having the fruit of the Spirit.

We turn now to the gifts of the Spirit.

Chapter Five

THE GIFTS OF THE SPIRIT

*To each is given the manifestation of the Spirit for the
common good. For to one is given through the Spirit
the utterance of wisdom, and to another the utterance
of knowledge according to the same Spirit, to another
faith by the same Spirit, to another gifts of healing by
the one Spirit, to another the working of miracles, to
another prophecy, to another the ability to distinguish
between spirits, to another various kinds of tongues,
to another the interpretation of tongues... helping,
administrating, and various kinds of tongues.*

—1 CORINTHIANS 12:7–10, 28

WHEREAS ALL BELIEVERS are commanded to manifest the *fruit* of the Spirit, the *gifts* of the Spirit are sovereignly bestowed on various people in the body of Christ by God. However, if you believe you are exempt from earnestly desiring the gifts of the Spirit, I answer: if you do not *want* them, I question whether you have the Holy Spirit at all. I firmly believe that if you have the Holy Spirit, you are going to welcome the pursuit of the *fruit* of the Spirit. Likewise, if you have the same Holy Spirit in you, you will take Paul's word seriously—to "covet" the *gifts* of the Spirit (1 Cor. 12:31, KJV).

The Greek word *zēloō* means "to burn with zeal" or "be zealous."[1] Paul uses this word in 1 Corinthians 12:31 to instruct us to be zealous in wanting the gifts of the Spirit. There is a scholarly debate whether *zēloō* is in the imperative mood—meaning a command; or if it is in the present tense, thus acknowledging what these Corinthians already coveted. Either way, it shows what people of the Spirit want—or should want!

The fruit of the Spirit is a demonstration to the world that we are different from the world. The world knows nothing of *agape* love, inner joy, and peace—not to mention self-control. The gifts of the Spirit are bestowed for our *effectiveness* in the world but also for *edifying* the body of Christ. The gifts are for the "common good" of the church (1 Cor. 12:7).

In my book *Holy Fire* I refute the notion that the gifts of the Spirit ceased (nobody knows when) centuries ago by God's decree. If that were so, the fruit of the Spirit should also cease! Thankfully neither ceased. If Jesus Christ is the same yesterday, today, and forever (Heb. 13:8), so too is the Holy Spirit—the same yesterday, today, and forever. God is the same. He does not change (Mal. 3:6). The commands of Scripture do not change. We are responsible for them all.

For example, when a new Christian begins reading the Bible, he or she will read it thinking that God is still all-powerful and can and does do anything! How sad when someone says to this new convert, "Oh, by the way, you can't believe all of the Bible." Liberals say that!

Why is it that Word people emphasize the fruit of the Spirit but seem to be shy when speaking of the gifts? I answer again: because of tongues. That's it. Nothing more. If there were no mention of the gift of tongues in 1 Corinthians 12, there would never have been a cessationist teaching. Tongues is where the offense is. My colleague Charles Carrin says, "It is the only gift that challenges our pride." There is no stigma when it comes to the other gifts—wisdom, knowledge, faith, miracles, prophecy. Who wouldn't welcome any of these? But because of *tongues*—which can be so embarrassing—one has to eliminate these greater gifts! And it is the greater gifts—the "higher gifts" (1 Cor. 12:31)—we are to earnestly desire.

Someone will no doubt say, "Since the gift of tongues is at the bottom of the list, that shows it is not important." Wrong. We just saw that self-control is at the bottom of Paul's list of the fruit of the Spirit—a very important fruit indeed. I do agree that wisdom is a higher gift than speaking in tongues—but *all* the gifts listed are important and valuable.

I say to anyone who wants as much of the Holy Spirit

as you can get: *be willing to start at the bottom—where the stigma is—if you really and truly want more of the Holy Spirit!* Do you want the gift of wisdom? Be willing to start at the bottom! Would you like the gift of healing? Be prepared to start at the bottom if you truly covet the gifts of the Holy Spirit as God's Word instructs you to.

Wisdom

This gift is first on Paul's list, and it is called "the utterance of wisdom" (1 Cor. 12:8). The King James Version says "word of wisdom." Whether this is a permanent bestowal on a person or if it is something that can be given once in an instance, either is possible. In other words, some may have a permanent gift and always show wisdom in what they say. Others may have a one-off utterance of wisdom when it was needed. *Utterance* comes from *logos*—word.

It is interesting that wisdom is not a fruit of the Spirit! It is also interesting that the original seven deacons were to be men "full of the Spirit *and* of wisdom" (Acts 6:3, emphasis added), suggesting that a person can be full of the Spirit and still not have wisdom. This notion does not surprise me; I have seen people who were full of the Spirit but very unwise!

Wisdom, then, is a gift of the Spirit. However, quite apart from being a gift of the Holy Spirit, wisdom is on offer to all. We are told to pray for wisdom, according to James 1:5. Furthermore, according to Proverbs 9:10, the way forward for wisdom is "the fear of the LORD." It has nothing to do with one's IQ or status.

The Greek word is *sophia*,[2] thought by the ancient Greeks to be out of reach for ordinary people. Only people such as

Plato, Socrates, and Aristotle could have *sophia*. The early Greeks were cessationists before their time!

However, the New Testament offers wisdom to *anyone*. Wisdom is having the presence of the mind of the Spirit. It is knowing what to do next—the next step forward in what God has in mind for you. It is 20/20 foresight vision. We all have 20/20 hindsight vision ("If only I had done that!"), but if you have the mind of the Holy Spirit, you will get it right in advance.

Wisdom is the paramount and supreme gift. *Get it*, "though it cost all you have" (Prov. 4:7, NIV). One could make a case that the first reference to prayer in the New Testament is to pray for wisdom. I say this because James is probably the first book in the New Testament to be written (AD 40–45). He immediately says, "If any of you lacks wisdom, let him ask God" (Jas. 1:5). We should, therefore, pray for the gift of wisdom and desire it above all the gifts.

> Prize her highly, and she will exalt you; she will honor you if you embrace her. She will place on your head a graceful garland; she will bestow on you a beautiful crown.
>
> —PROVERBS 4:8–9

It is the highest, greatest, and most important gift. The apostles had it in the early church and required it of the seven original deacons. Paul lists it first when mentioning the gifts of the Holy Spirit.

Knowledge

It is called "utterance of knowledge" in the English Standard Version, "word of knowledge" in the King James Version, and "message of knowledge" in the New International Version.

The phrase "word of knowledge" has become quite popular among many Charismatic believers. Using the language of the King James Version, rightly or wrongly, they often refer to "a word of knowledge" in much the same way as a prophetic word. I'm not saying it is incorrect to apply the phrase "word of knowledge" in a manner closely akin to the gift of prophecy. Many of the gifts of the Spirit border on each other, as in healing and miracles.

There is a difference between wisdom and knowledge. Wisdom is not necessarily knowledge; knowledge is certainly not necessarily wisdom. People can have extraordinary knowledge but sorely lack wisdom. Wisdom is the way you *use* or *apply* the knowledge you have. Knowledge may be a storage of facts or information. Some people know many facts; some have a lot of information. Could this be the right understanding of an utterance of knowledge? Possibly. God could in a moment of need call on such a person to give a timely word based upon years of study.

We should connect all these gifts with the concept of "common grace"—special grace in nature. All of humankind have a level of common grace. It is called "common" not because it is ordinary but because it is given commonly to all—whether or not you get saved. Common grace refers to the natural abilities you received in the way God made you, whether or not you become a Christian. At the level of common grace is your intelligence, your capacity to acquire and retain knowledge, your memory, and the genetic tendencies you inherited from your parents.

It is my observation that gifts of the Spirit sometimes connect to one's natural abilities. For example, once redeemed through salvation in Christ, people who have natural shrewdness or good judgment are likely to have the gift of wisdom. In other words, if a naturally clever person becomes a Christian, it should not be surprising that he or she has the gift of the utterance of wisdom. It is the same with the gift of the utterance of knowledge.

The word *knowledge* comes from *gnosis*—sometimes referring to revealed knowledge, vis-à-vis *oida*, which generally means knowledge of facts.[3] *Gnosis* would fit well with the way "word of knowledge" is often used by Charismatics. They sometimes have words of knowledge revealed to them by the Spirit.

Could an utterance of knowledge refer to a person's intellect and wealth of knowledge? Possibly. A person highly learned but filled with the Spirit may have a message of knowledge based upon what they have accumulated over the years. This would also show how common grace figures in the gifts. A person with a vast knowledge of the Bible might also deliver an utterance of knowledge—whether on a one-to-one basis or from a pulpit to many.

To summarize: the gift of the utterance of knowledge may have more than one meaning and have more than one application.

Faith

This gift of the Spirit can be puzzling. If we are justified—saved—by faith, why would Paul list faith as a gift of the Spirit?

There are two kinds of faith, generally speaking. First, there is saving faith. This kind of faith justifies; it redeems. This faith assures you of a home in Heaven when you die. It comes by transferring the trust you once had in your good works to what Jesus did for you by His death. It is when you believe you are saved through Christ alone.

Second, there is persistent faith. This faith leads to your inheritance. All Christians are called to come into their inheritance. Some do; some don't. Those who do will not only come into an inheritance in this life but also receive a reward at the judgment seat of Christ (1 Cor. 3:14; 2 Cor. 5:10). Those who do not persist in faith not only blow away the inheritance they could have had on earth but will forfeit a reward at the judgment seat of Christ (1 Cor. 3:15).

Those described in Hebrews 11 are men and women with persistent faith. Hebrews 11 is not about saving faith; it is about people who persevered and accomplished great things for God—those "of whom the world was not worthy" (v. 38).

Which type of faith does Paul list with the gifts of the Spirit? It is not saving faith; he is writing to Christians who are already saved. It certainly could be persistent faith such as the faith that described Abraham, Isaac, Jacob, Joseph, Moses, and others.

However, I believe there may be a third category for this faith given as a gift of the Spirit—a faith given for a special circumstance or a particular situation. You might receive faith that someone you are praying for will get saved. You might receive faith for answered prayer: "If we know that he hears us in whatever we ask, we know that we have the requests that we have asked of him" (1 John 5:15). That is a big "if"—knowing that the Most High has heard us. But God may grant this faith for a special occasion to you.

George Müller (1805–1898) of Bristol, England, was known as a "man of faith." He lived by faith, observing God daily, month after month, to send in funds and food to the orphanage he founded. Curiously, he denied having the gift of faith! I think, however, he did have it.

Dr. Lloyd-Jones told me of a man who received unusual faith—or perhaps it was a word of knowledge—during the Welsh Revival of 1904. The man had a ministry to the poor and homeless. During the height of the Welsh Revival, this man was given knowledge of the exact number of home- less people who would be at breakfast the next day, and the food always came in for that exact number.

When the Welsh Revival subsided, the man stopped having this phenomenon. Dr. Lloyd-Jones knew him and had to counsel him. The man went into a depression; he feared he had done something wrong that caused this to stop.

The gift of faith is probably best understood as special faith for a particular occasion.

Healing

All of us could certainly wish for this gift. As I write these lines, my wife, Louise, is waiting for a second opera- tion on her back—a herniated disc. The pain she has expe- rienced is the worst of our sixty years of marriage. I have prayed for her dozens and dozens and dozens of times. No healing.

However, on a different occasion, I put my hands on the temples of a Scottish woman whom I had never met before and prayed for her at her request. She wrote months later to say she had sinus headaches for five years, but that day I prayed for her was the worst of her life. "When you prayed, I felt nothing," she wrote. "But a few hours later I realized the pain was gone and never came back." Does that mean I have the gift of healing? No. I didn't even have faith for her healing! I too felt nothing. I was in a hurry. I stopped to pray for her out of courtesy, but God overruled my lack of faith and healed this woman.

Perhaps you see by now that there is an element of mystery in the gifts of the Spirit. I don't fully understand any of them! We can only do our best to grasp what the Holy Spirit is teaching. I have learned this much: *don't try to figure God out.*

Do some people have a permanent gift of healing? Possibly. Oral Roberts (1918–2009)—whom I met three times in his house in California—comes the closest to anybody I know of who had this gift. There are no doubt thousands of people with little or no profile who have—at least at times—a gift of healing. It is a mystery.

Those few people healed under my ministry—so far—were a complete surprise to me. On no occasion when I have prayed for people did I "feel" faith that God would heal them. The most spectacular convert of my ministry at Westminster Chapel—a Muslim woman from Turkey then living in London—was healed of throat cancer within a few days after I prayed for her. I don't even remember praying for her! She told me I did.

The working of miracles

This gift is equally mysterious. Does this refer to healing or a sudden miracle of a rather spectacular nature—such as a person delivered of demon possession? My friend Charles Carrin tells of a time when a dangerous storm front—potentially a tornado—was headed for Florence, Alabama, while he was preaching in a service there. He prayed that the storm would bypass the church building. Moments after Charles prayed, the storm split—half of it went to the south, half to the north—completely avoiding the church premises. The split storm then came back together on the other side of the church building. This activity appeared on the radar screen, and people there still talk about it. That event surely qualifies as a miracle.

Sometimes healings are also called miracles. Supernatural healings are miracles, but not all miracles are healings.

In my book *Holy Fire* I related an experience I had regarding demon possession, which I shall share here. A new convert named Tony revealed he had attended a black mass. He claimed he felt razors cutting his stomach. Taking my cue from the wisdom of Dr. Lloyd-Jones, I began saying, "Jesus Christ is come in the flesh, Jesus Christ is come in the flesh, Jesus Christ is come in the flesh," several times until he looked utterly terrified. I then said, "In the name of Jesus Christ, come out of him and go to the place of your appointment and do not return." Tony collapsed and went completely limp. I helped him walk to a place where he could sit. Several minutes later Tony walked on his own steam, and his countenance went from ashen gray to a normal color. "I don't know what you did, but I feel so good inside," he said to me.

On another occasion I confronted the demonic when I prayed for a man who could not sleep well. He said his mother was a witch; he had not had a decent night's sleep in twenty-five years. "The spirits keep kicking me out of bed," he said. A deacon and I anointed him with oil and prayed. We did not try to cast a demon out. I felt nothing.

However, the following Sunday he said, "I slept three full nights this week. Would you have another go?" We prayed again for him. He returned the following Sunday stating he had seven full nights' sleep, adding, "I slept like a baby."

I waited six months before I asked him to give his testimony—sadly owing to my lack of faith. His was probably a case of deliverance from the demonic, but I am not sure how to categorize it. I call it a miracle, and I wish I saw this sort of thing more often.

Prophecy

This gift is one Paul especially wanted the Corinthians to have. "Pursue love, and especially desire the spiritual gifts, especially that you may prophesy" (1 Cor. 14:1). The gift of prophecy is the ability to unveil God's will for the church at a given moment. It is not an invitation to be another Elijah, Isaiah, or Jeremiah. The apostles were successors to these major men in the Old Testament. There are levels of prophecy, which I will explain further in a later chapter.

I do not mean to say God cannot raise up sovereign

vessels—other than apostles—who have a special gift of declaring the immediate word of God. Luke mentions Agabus (Acts 11:27–28; 21:10–12) as having the gift of prophecy. However, I should point out too that Agabus' prophecy regarding Paul going to Jerusalem, though generally fulfilled, was not fulfilled in every detail. This fact alone is a strong hint that New Testament prophecy was not expected to be on the same level as the canonical prophets of the Old Testament.

The gift of prophecy in the New Testament was for the local church. When people came together to worship, some people would offer a prophetic word that edified the body of Christ. The Corinthians made the mistake—often repeated today—of thinking speaking in tongues was everything. The Corinthians relished their speaking in tongues—which no one understood. Paul rebuked them soundly, stating: "I would rather speak five words with my mind in order to instruct others, than ten thousand words in a tongue" (1 Cor. 14:19).

We must test any prophetic word. "Do not despise prophecies, but test everything; hold fast what is good" (1 Thess. 5:20–21).

There were often hard times when we were at Westminster Chapel. One situation had to do with our family; certain people in the church had been cruel regarding one of our children. One Sunday morning Louise went to the chapel with a very heavy heart. As soon as she arrived, a Nigerian woman named Grace, who had been waiting for Louise, came to her with a prophetic word. She said *one single word* to Louise, a word Louise knew immediately was from the Lord. It gave her tremendous comfort.

That is an example of the gift of prophecy in the church.

The ability to distinguish between spirits

To distinguish between spirits means primarily to know the difference between the Holy Spirit and a demonic spirit.

It is a timely reminder that we are in a war with Satan. He hates Jesus Christ, who is his prime enemy, and also those who are *in* Christ. Satan has our number and will do *anything* to shake us, divert us, deceive us, or oppress us. It is important therefore to know the enemy. However, you must know the real thing before you can recognize the counterfeit.

This gift is valuable. We need to be able to see what is real and genuine and what is not. As I explained in *Pigeon Religion*, the dove is the authentic symbol of the Holy Spirit; the pigeon is the counterfeit. Remember, doves and pigeons are in the same family. Anatomically they are identical, but temperamentally they are different. I have heard people say, "The Holy Ghost came down," but when you get to the bottom of it, it is sometimes what I call pigeon religion. It's worth mentioning that pigeon religion can be a fleshly counterfeit and not necessarily demonic.

The first task, then, is to be able to recognize the true Holy Spirit. He is the true Spirit of God, the third person of the Trinity. I think many sincere Christians immediately and hastily focus on the demonic when applying this particular gift of the Spirit. Do not make this mistake. Our first responsibility is to be able to know and discern the *true presence of God*. As I said, we must know the *real* before we can recognize the counterfeit. It is a big mistake to focus on the counterfeit and become an "expert" in demonology. I have known people who thrive on books about the occult, witchcraft, and demons. Such people always strike me as not being very spiritual or godly.

John said we must "test the spirits to see whether they are from God" (1 John 4:1). He gave this instruction because there are false prophets around. "Every spirit that confesses that Jesus Christ has come in the flesh is from God" (v. 2). When I was asked to give my opinion of the Toronto Blessing, a revival that took place at the Toronto Airport Vineyard back in 1994, I began with 1 John 4:1–4. As I will show further later, it became obvious to me that what was abroad in the Toronto church was the true Holy Spirit: the people there—from John Arnott to the leadership—passed this test.

You might be asking, "But, R. T., could there not be much of the flesh in such a move of God?" Yes. Even if one discerns that the Holy Spirit is truly at work, one can expect the flesh to be present. It always is—as in the case of the Great Awakening of the eighteenth century. Even George Whitefield (1714–1770), one of the primary leaders in this move of the Spirit, sadly did things that were of the flesh.

These things said, the first task is to know how to discern the Holy Spirit of God. If one has the ability to recognize the Holy Spirit, it becomes relatively easy to discern the demonic. The contrast will be obvious. However, if you *begin* trying to spot the demonic, you may miss seeing what is going on. You must begin with a solid and sound understanding of the person and presence of the Holy Spirit. Then the demonic—if present—will saliently manifest.

However, having the ability to see the demonic does not mean one also has the gift to cast out demons. Casting out demons is sometimes a separate gift, possibly coming under the gift pertaining to miracles. I say more about this in my book *Holy Fire*, relating an account when I personally cast out a demon. But I must also say I have only done it once (so far).

Various kinds of tongues

Tongue—meaning language—is a translation of the Greek *glossa*. The modern Charismatic movement began in the 1960s. As I will show further later, it was initially known as the glossolalia movement, owing to the emphasis on speaking in tongues.

Until 1960 it was primarily Pentecostals, having their origin in the Azusa Street revival in Los Angeles (1906), who were associated with speaking in tongues. They were mainly found in the Elim Church (a United Kingdom-based Pentecostal denomination), the Assemblies of God, the Pentecostal Holiness Church, the Church of God, and the Church of God of Prophecy.

The Charismatic movement, as it is named, began decades later when a growing number of churches in mainline denominations suddenly encountered and embraced what were thought of as Pentecostal experiences. The new movement included Episcopalians, Baptists, Presbyterians, Reformed, and others—including Roman Catholics. The word *charismatic* comes from the Greek *charismata*—meaning "grace-gift."[4] As the name indicates, *all* gifts of the Spirit—not merely tongues—were given recognition in the new movement.

"Various kinds of tongues," then, means different languages (1 Cor. 12:10). The inauguration of this gift came on the day of Pentecost when 120 disciples were filled with the Spirit and "began to speak in other tongues as the Spirit gave them utterance" (Acts 2:4). They were baptized with the Holy Spirit as Jesus had announced: "You will be baptized with the Holy Spirit not many days from now" (Acts 1:5).

For this reason most Pentecostals and Charismatics hold that you will speak with tongues if you are baptized with the Spirit; that if you don't speak with tongues, you have not been baptized with the Spirit. But not all of us agree with this. I am convinced that what happened to me on October 31, 1955, was the baptism of the Holy Spirit. Some four months later I spoke in tongues, however. I say more about this in *Holy Fire*.

That said, the 120 disciples spoke with "other tongues"— languages not their own. Moreover, people from foreign nations *heard* the disciples speaking in *their* language. "Each one was hearing them speak in his own language" (Acts 2:6). It was a double miracle: they spoke in other tongues and were heard by foreigners in their own language!

There has been much discussion about whether a person who receives a "heavenly language" experiences exactly what happened to the 120 on the day of Pentecost. Some say yes; some say no. I lean to the latter because the "heavenly language" is almost always a case of speaking unintelligible sounds that no one understands. Although the tongues phenomenon certainly began at Pentecost, it would not seem that praying in the Spirit—when one "speaks not to men but to God"—is the same thing; "for no one understands him, but he utters mysteries in the Spirit" (1 Cor. 14:2).

This is why Paul speaks of "various kinds of tongues." I see at least three possibilities: (1) one speaks in some *known* language—at least known to some people somewhere on the planet; (2) it is a unique language—no one understands the person, which is what 1 Corinthians 14:2 refers to; or (3) it is an angelic language—literally the untranslated tongue of angels. This could be why Paul refers to "the tongues of men and of angels" (1 Cor. 13:1).

I admit to being curious about what I must be saying when I pray in tongues (which I often do). Paul says I utter "mysteries in the Spirit" (1 Cor. 14:2). My greatest blessing comes from knowing that although I don't know what I'm saying, the Spirit takes over and intercedes according to the will of God. Paul speaks of this:

> For we do not know what to pray for as we ought, but the Spirit himself intercedes for us with groanings too deep for words. And he who searches hearts knows what is the mind of the Spirit, because the Spirit intercedes for the saints according to the will of God.
>
> —ROMANS 8:26–27

A friend of mine studied with Dr. Bruce Metzger (1914–2007), a professor at Princeton Theological Seminary and one of the greatest Greek scholars and textual critics of our time. My friend asked Dr. Metzger, "Was Paul referring to praying in tongues in Romans 8:26–27?"

Metzger—a Presbyterian and possibly a cessationist—replied, "Of course he was."

The interpretation of tongues

This gift implies that there *is* an interpretation of any tongue uttered by the power of the Holy Spirit. In other words, speaking or praying in tongues is not meaningless. Some people are enabled by the Spirit to speak in various tongues; others are able to interpret what they said. Paul admonished the Corinthians not to speak in tongues in a gathering where visitors would have no clue what was said. If one does speak in tongues publicly, it is fine—that is, as long as someone has the interpretation.

> If any speak in a tongue, let there be only two or at most three, and each in turn, and let someone interpret. But if there is no one to interpret, let each of them keep silent in church and speak to himself and to God.
>
> —1 CORINTHIANS 14:27–28

The problem often encountered is when people give their *own* interpretation of the message in tongues that they themselves just uttered. This may seem benign, but it is suspect. It was not what Paul had in mind. He wanted someone who had the gift of interpretation to step in and interpret. When the same person gives the interpretation, it lacks credibility and authenticity.

There was a sweet old man who would come to Westminster Chapel on Sunday evenings and utter a tongue—lasting less than a minute—during communion. The first time he did, it seemed harmless. But the following communion service he did it again. And again. And again. The curious thing was, the interpretation was always the same, something like this: "Thus saith the Lord, I am with you, will guide you, bless you, look after you"—or something like that. Every time. People began to dread communion service because they feared this man would stand up and do the same again. It did not edify anybody. I finally gave a gentle word to him that speaking in such a manner did not edify people. He was deeply offended and never came back.

Pastor Jack Hayford tells the story of being on a plane when he felt led to utter a tongue to the person sitting next to him. He dreaded doing it and tried to avoid it, but it was on him so strong that he gave in and uttered a strange set of syllables he did not understand. However, the man next to him was an Indian, who turned to Jack to say, "You have just said words that only my tribe speaks!" It was a wonderful testimony. There are many stories like this where a person spoke in a language he or she did not understand, but foreigners were astonished to recognize their own language!

Once, when we were living in Key Largo, Florida, I sat on the porch overlooking Largo Sound, and the following happened to me. I was praying and uttered a tongue when I immediately heard these words: "Stop taking yourself so seriously." I am sure it was an instantaneous interpretation—and a loving rebuke that I needed.

The gift of interpretation of tongues is—I think—rare. For that matter, perhaps all the genuine gifts of the Spirit are rare these days. I am no cessationist. However, I think we give our critics credibility when we tolerate the counterfeit without "proving all things." I fear that some of us are so anxious to see God work that we try to *make* things happen—whether trying to prove that someone is healed when they are not healed or uttering prophecies that never come true.

The greatest freedom is having nothing to prove.

PART II:
THE TRUTH OF
THE WORD

Chapter Six

CAN WE HAVE THE SPIRIT WITHOUT THE WORD?

Are you so foolish? Having begun by the Spirit,
are you now being perfected by the flesh?

—GALATIANS 3:3

You may recall the quote by A. W. Tozer (1897–1963) at the beginning of this book that included these words: "It is never possible to have the Spirit without at least some measure of truth."[1] This is because the Holy Spirit is the "Spirit *of truth*, who proceeds from the Father" (John 15:26, emphasis added). There is a sense in which the essence of God is *truth*. For example:

- "It is impossible for God to lie" (Heb. 6:18).

- Indeed, God "never lies" (Titus 1:2).

- David prayed, "Lead me in your truth and teach me" (Ps. 25:5).

- "All his works are done in truth" (Ps. 33:4, kjv).

- "Send out your light and your truth" (Ps. 43:3).

- "Your law is true" (Ps. 119:142).

- "All your commandments are true" (Ps. 119:151).

- "The Lord is near to all who call on him, to all who call on him in truth" (Ps. 145:18).

- "So that he who blesses himself in the land shall bless himself by the God of truth, and he who takes an oath in the land shall swear by the God of truth" (Isa. 65:16).

- "I will tell you what is inscribed in the book of truth" (Dan. 10:21).

The same applies to Jesus Christ:

- "We have seen his glory, the glory as of the only Son from the Father, full of grace and truth" (John 1:14).

- "For the law was given through Moses, grace and truth came through Jesus Christ" (John 1:17).

- "And you will know the truth, and the truth will set you free" (John 8:32).

- "If I tell you the truth, why do you not believe me?" (John 8:46).

- "I am the way, and the truth, and the life. No one comes to the Father except through me" (John 14:6).

To me, the truth *about* God and the truth *of* God and the truth *from* God are among the most dazzling, breathtaking, and thrilling things about God. This is why He has "magnified" His Word above all His name (Ps. 138:2, KJV)! His Word is truth. Jesus prayed, "Sanctify them in the truth; your word is truth" (John 17:17).

The Welsh Revival, which I've mentioned previously, was one of the great moves of the Holy Spirit in modern church history. Estimates of the number of people converted range from twenty-five thousand to fifty thousand. The pubs and jails emptied. Bethan Phillips was a six-year-old living in London when her father took her out of school and put her on a train to Wales. Members of the family criticized him for taking her out of school. His reply: "She can always go to school, but she may never see revival again."

Bethan grew up and married Dr. Martyn Lloyd-Jones. Years later, in her eighties, she spoke with me about that time, recalling when she personally witnessed the Welsh Revival. Dr. Lloyd-Jones also told me this story:

> A coal miner came home from work, and his wife had not cooked his dinner. She had gone to the church to be in the revival. He was so livid and upset that he decided to go to the church and stop the revival. When he arrived, he could not get into the building as people were crowding the door. Refusing to be kept out, he angrily elbowed his way through the people into the church. The next thing he remembers is being on his knees in front of the pulpit, crying to God for mercy! Those who witnessed the event said that he managed to get inside the church and literally stepped on the top of the back pew then made his way to the front by stepping on the top of every pew. He then fell before the pulpit and began praying.

Serious critics of the Welsh Revival said this phenomenon could not be of God because of the absence of preaching. The previously mentioned Evan Roberts did not preach but sat on the platform. Some would, therefore, argue against the statement of Tozer that "it is never possible to have the Spirit without at least some measure of truth." One concluded that the Welsh Revival disproved Tozer's statement since the revival had little or no preaching but all singing, showing that this movement was not a work of the Spirit.

I reply: What exactly did they sing during that epochal

era? If it were a false spirit but not the Holy Spirit, one would expect that the hymns would be strange, heretical, and unbiblical. This was not the case! They sang the biblical hymns of the church! In all the churches virtually every evening the most popular and most frequent hymn was this:

> Here is love, vast as the ocean,
> Loving-kindness as the flood,
> When the Prince of Life, our Ransom,
> Shed for us His precious blood.
> Who His love will not remember?
> Who can cease to sing His praise?
> He can never be forgotten
> Throughout heav'n's eternal days.
>
> On the mount of crucifixion
> Fountains open deep and wide;
> Through the floodgates of God's mercy
> Flowed a vast and gracious tide.
> Grace and love, like mighty rivers,
> Poured incessant from above,
> And heav'n's peace and perfect justice
> Kissed a guilty world in love.
>
> In Thy truth Thou dost direct me
> By Thy Spirit through Thy Word;
> And Thy grace my need is meeting
> As I trust in Thee, my Lord.
> Of Thy fullness Thou art pouring
> Thy great love and pow'r on me,
> Without measure, full and boundless,
> Drawing out my heart to Thee.[2]
>   —WILLIAM REES (1802–1883)

The early Methodists got their theology from their hymns. Examine the hymns of people such as Isaac Watts (1674–1748) and Charles Wesley. The content of these God-honoring hymns was theologically sound and used by the Holy Spirit not only to edify the saints but also to convict the lost. Preaching can be sung as easily as it is spoken.

Think about this. What if the God who exists were an untruthful God? What if He lied? What if He could not be believed? What if He were not faithful? He did not say, "I will turn myself into a God of truth." He did not say, "I will be truthful." Nor did He say, "I will always tell the truth." No. He *is* truth. It is impossible for Him not to be truthful. The everlasting God *is a God of truth*. He is a God of honesty and integrity. He is a God who is faithful and keeps His Word! You can fully trust Him. As we saw in Frances Havergal's hymn in a previous chapter, "They who trust Him wholly find Him wholly true."

This easily brings me to tears. What a wonderful God we have! How blessed can we be? It doesn't get better than this.

Therefore, if one begins in the Spirit, it is because *truth* was present.

However, the Galatians sadly wandered from the truth. Not totally. Even in their weakened condition, they had a measure of truth.

The issue? The Gospel. It often is. This is why I wrote the book *Whatever Happened to the Gospel?* (Charisma House). Paul was alarmed at what was happening to his converts at Galatia. He corresponded with deepest urgency: "I am astonished that you are so quickly deserting him who called you in the grace of Christ and are turning to a different gospel—not that there is another one, but there are some who trouble you and want to distort the gospel of Christ" (Gal. 1:6–7).

It is worth noting that Paul does not question their conversions. There might be some today who would say that if the Galatians' conversions were genuine, they would not have been so quickly influenced by false teaching. Quite the contrary; Paul does all he can to sort them out lest they be demoralized and disillusioned. The reason for Paul's letters—that form almost a third of the New Testament—is because all converts need teaching and often warning.

Judaizers (as we now call them)—Jews who professed to be Christians—had deceived the Galatians. Their predominant motive was to persuade Paul's Gentile converts to embrace the whole of the Mosaic Law, including circumcision. These Judaizers only fished in the Christian pond; they followed Paul almost wherever he went and lived to detract his converts. Some scholars suggest that the Judaizers might have been Paul's "thorn in the flesh" (see 2 Cor. 12:7).

These Judaizers appeared to succeed with the Galatians to a considerable extent. Although converted through Paul, the Galatians turned against him. Paul did his best to wake them up and bring them back to the truth of the Gospel. "Have I then become your enemy by telling you the truth?" he asked (Gal. 4:16).

Paul, therefore, put this to them, "Having begun by the Spirit, are you now being perfected by the flesh?" (Gal. 3:3). This further shows they had been converted: they began by the Spirit. By "flesh" here Paul means embracing the Law. Although the Law is *truth*, they wandered from the truth by misunderstanding the *place* of the Law in God's purpose. Paul reminds them that the Gospel was first preached to Abraham (Gal. 3:8), that they were justified by faith like Abraham was. The Law came in 430 years *later* (Gal. 3:17). In other words, the covenant we are now under is *not* the Mosaic Law but rather the one given to Abraham!

The Galatians had almost certainly never given these things any thought. Paul knew the Law far better than the Judaizers did. The Judaizers told these Gentile Galatians that Paul had let them down. Paul had to step in and teach them elementary things—most importantly, to show that Jesus' death on the cross had fulfilled the Law. This puts us back to Abraham!

Owing to the pernicious influence of these Judaizers, then, the Galatians had wandered far from the truth! Paul spoon-feeds them in his letter to them with the purpose that Christ be formed in them (Gal. 4:19). "You have fallen away from grace," that is, they were living beneath the grace that was rightfully theirs (Gal. 5:4). They were being cheated by listening to these Jews. Although Paul said he had "confidence in the Lord" that the Galatians would come to their senses (Gal. 5:10), we won't know until we get to Heaven how these Galatians turned out!

This event shows how saved people can have the Holy Spirit but not necessarily possess a high level of truth. Although these Galatians were saved, they had become vulnerable to heresy. They were not upholding the Gospel that saved them. Furthermore, by their listening to the Judaizers, the offense of the cross was removed (Gal. 5:11).

Like many churches today throughout the world, the Galatians had the Spirit but only a measure of truth, to refer to Tozer's comment. There is no reason to believe that they abandoned the essentials of the faith such as the deity and humanity of Jesus, His bodily resurrection and ascension. As long as one believes in Jesus as the God-man and His resurrection from the dead, he is saved (Rom. 10:9–10). Even if you say, "saved but only just," I would agree, but saved they were, and that is the essential truth we must not forget.

This explains how a church—or a minister—can have the Holy Spirit but lack in sound theology. Indeed, the Holy Spirit on people can do extraordinary things—e.g., preach impressive sermons, write good music and poetry, or be instruments in healing, lively worship, true deliverances, and remarkable prophecies. What is more, as we have seen, the gifts of the Spirit are irrevocable (Rom. 11:29)—meaning that (1) you do not lose them, and (2) personal holiness does not guarantee they will be granted. The anointing comes by the sovereign will of God. Never forget that King Saul prophesied on his way to kill David (1 Sam. 19:24). When God said, "I...will show mercy to whom I will show mercy" (Exod. 33:19; see also Rom. 9:15), this means that He withholds judgment on those of us who deserve judgment. The difference between grace and mercy is this: grace is receiving favor we *don't* deserve; mercy is having God withhold justice we *do* deserve.

This also means God has mercy on those who are not

always theologically correct. This lesson teaches those of us who wrongly assume that our sound theology scores points with God. God might choose to bypass those of us who fancy ourselves to be "sound" in doctrine, and He might bless those who—at the moment—may not have a great measure of truth!

I referred earlier to having Arthur Blessitt at Westminster Chapel. He does not pretend to be a theologian, but I knew he was a man who loved God and was willing to throw his reputation to the wind to obey God. I wanted a man like that around for a while. However, some good people were puzzled that I invited Arthur. One person wrote to ask me why I was "settling for Ishmael," noting that long ago I had said the Charismatic movement was Ishmael, but Isaac was coming. I possibly lost more friends over having Arthur than any decision I ever made, but it was the best decision I made in twenty-five years at Westminster Chapel.

One day in 1994, I received a phone call from Ken Costa, churchwarden of Holy Trinity Brompton (HTB), a prominent Anglican church in London (now the largest in England), also known to be open to the Holy Spirit. Ken said to me, "Some unusual things are happening in our church, and I am wondering if you have any sermons on 1 John 4:1–4?" Yes. I immediately sent him four sermons on those verses that deal with testing the spirits to see whether they were of God. After Ken read those sermons, he asked to take me to lunch to talk about what was going on at HTB. I went to lunch to warn him. Several days before, I had heard about people being prayed for and falling down with laughter. People said this came from Toronto.

I initially doubted that such was of God. I certainly didn't want to think it was of God. I found that sort of thing disturbing!

Also, if I am totally candid, I felt a little bit betrayed by God. After all, if what was going on at HTB was indeed from the Holy Spirit, if it was genuinely of God, it would surely have come to Westminster Chapel first! I struggled to believe that He would bless HTB and not Westminster Chapel! I considered the Church of England apostate. "Surely God would not bless a church with all those Etonians on their staff," I thought, "with their posh Sloan Square accents!" We at Westminster Chapel were ordinary Christians as described in 1 Corinthians 1:26–31. Jealousy is a hard sin to see in ourselves.

There was more. I had faithfully upheld the historic Gospel against severe opposition and had become vulnerable by having an Arthur Blessitt turn us upside down. Furthermore, our church had days of prayer and fasting. I was out on the streets witnessing to the lost. I am ashamed to say that I assumed that God would surely favor us over Anglican churches, including HTB.

Ken had not come to persuade me of what was going on in his church. He sincerely wanted my opinion. But halfway through that lunch, I became extremely concerned that, just maybe, I was opposing a work of God merely because it did not come to us first. I recalled how many Christians opposed the Welsh Revival. I knew there was a very long tradition that resisted what God was doing in certain generations. I truly began to fear that I might be on the wrong side.

There was also a glow on Ken's face that began to give me pause. Not only that, but HTB clearly passed the test of 1 John 4:1–4. They may or may not have been as Reformed as I was, but neither was John Wesley!

By the time we finished lunch, I was sobered from head to toe. I phoned Louise to tell her I believed I had been wrong with regard to the Toronto Blessing. I called my deacons together to say the same thing. To their credit, they stood with me. I had warned my congregation at Westminster weeks before of what was going on at HTB, but after that lunch with Ken, I publicly took it back. I am so glad I did.

Later that year my wife, Louise, was miraculously healed in seconds by a man who is known to be the "father" of the Toronto Blessing. Louise came into the chapel vestry that Saturday morning, having slept little the night before. She admits that she had no faith but was willing to let "that man" (she did not know who he was) pray for her. She was instantly healed. I can pick that man's theology to pieces! He became a dear friend and will vouch how I have pleaded with him to get sorted out on certain issues. I still pray that he will come around. I could refer to many others who see miracles but are not what I personally regard as "sound." There are those whose theology (surely) must make the angels blush but whom God uses amazingly.

When God said, "I will have mercy on whom I will have mercy," He meant just that. He is sovereign and shows mercy to whom He will—whether to a church or an individual. Why? Because that is the way He is.

The God of the Bible is a God of truth. The truth is,

He sometimes blesses those that you and I would never choose. He bypasses those that you and I would assume to be exactly where God would manifest His glory next.

I love the story behind one of Fanny Crosby's best-known songs. I read that she was addressing some prisoners in a jail one Sunday afternoon. She had reason to quote Romans 9:15, "I will have mercy on whom I will have mercy," noting that God has a right to pass by people. A prisoner cried out, "O Lord, don't pass by me." She went home and wrote the hymn:

> Pass me not O gentle Savior,
> Hear my humble cry;
> While on others Thou art calling,
> Do not pass me by.[3]
>   —FANNY CROSBY (1820–1915)

It has been my privilege to preach at the Toronto church a number of times. But I want to share what happened on my first visit there—in 1996, on the second anniversary of the Toronto Blessing. I prayed all day long to know what I should preach on at the evening meeting. I came up with nothing.

I decided at the last minute to use an old sermon I have preached perhaps hundreds of times based on Hebrews 4:14–16. I knew that sermon backward and forward, but when I began reading the text to the congregation, I struggled just to read it out loud. A heaviness came on me that kept me from finishing a sentence! Never in my life had I experienced anything like this. I could not put two sentences together.

As I tried and tried, the congregation (perhaps two thousand) began to laugh hilariously. Louise on the second row was laughing. Lyndon Bowring, sitting next to her, was laughing his head off. It wasn't funny to me. I began to think, "What will they say back in England when they hear that I—known to be a Bible teacher—could not even preach when at the Toronto church? The critics will say this is proof that the whole thing is not of God."

I was feeling panicky. There was no joy. I prayed like mad: "Please, Lord, help me." I was helpless for about fifteen minutes, although it seemed like an eternity. I could not put together an intelligible sentence. If someone had offered me one million tax-free dollars in gold bullion to preach my sermon, I could not have done it.

Mercifully a different verse came to mind; I sensed Hebrews 13:13, not knowing what it said. I turned to it and wondered if this is what I should speak on: "Let us, then, go to him outside the camp, bearing the disgrace he bore" (NIV). I then announced to the crowd, "I will try a different text." They laughed again, but when I began to read, the atmosphere suddenly changed; you could almost hear a pin drop. I began to speak—to soar. I preached for perhaps twenty minutes about Jesus dying on the cross outside the city and that we all must go outside the camp, bearing His reproach. Many came forward—some say two hundred or more—when I finished. I have had people come up to me from different parts of the world to say, "I was there that night and came forward after you preached."

But there is more to the story. That sermon on Hebrews 13:13 was the first sermon preached in the Toronto Airport

Christian Fellowship! Until the very day before it was the Toronto Airport Vineyard. It is well-known that the late John Wimber (1934–1997), the founder of Vineyard—a man I knew fairly well and liked a lot—disenfranchised the Toronto church for some reason. He also later regretted doing so. He said to several people just days before he went to Heaven, "It was the worst mistake of my life."[4] In any case, the day I preached from Hebrews 13:13 was the first day it had ceased to be a Vineyard church. My sermon was the first to be preached at the church with its new name. The Toronto congregation was literally outside the camp! God knew that they needed encouragement.

The above incident shows me two things. First, my sermon on Hebrews 4:16 was not what God wanted me to preach; He wanted me to affirm the Toronto church that had been disenfranchised and made to go outside the camp. Second, it showed how the Holy Spirit took over that night. It was utterly out of my hands. I was literally *unable* to preach what I tried to preach. I have done my best in these lines to explain what happened. It was physically impossible for me to speak until I heard Hebrews 13:13.

The Toronto pastor John Arnott and his lovely wife, Carol, have become great friends to Louise and me. I have linked up with them in ministry several times in different parts of the world. I affirm them, and they affirm me although, for all I know, we possibly don't always dot i's or cross t's the same way. And yet maybe we do!

On the day following my talks at the first Word and Spirit Conference in Wembley Conference Centre in 1992, a well-known church leader phoned to ask me this: "By

'Word' do you mean 'Reformed'?" I knew exactly what he meant. I asked him for time to think about that. I now conclude that if Dr. Lloyd-Jones could lean on John Wesley to support his own doctrine of the Holy Spirit—Wesley not being Reformed—there is my answer. I would be unfair to require everyone to be Reformed in theology in their efforts to be Word people as well as Spirit people. God has a wider net than some of us to pull in those He chooses to bless.

The presence of the Holy Spirit—the Spirit of truth—can manifest in amazing ways, indeed manifesting *in* those and to those you and I might think have but a small measure of truth. Paul did not give up on the Galatians. We must not give up on one another who sincerely and earnestly seek the honor and glory of God.

Chapter Seven

LOGOS AND RHEMA

Thou hast magnified thy word above all thy name.

—PSALM 138:2, KJV

THE VERSE THAT opens this chapter is extraordinary. Please read it again. When you think how God wants His name to be honored, think about this: He magnifies His Word above all His name.

Knowing that modern translations strangely gloss over this verse—interpreting rather than translating—I began to wonder if maybe the King James Version got it wrong, although the English Standard Version has a footnote: "You have exalted your word above all your name." I asked the late Dr. Michael Eaton (1942–2017), one of the most learned men I have ever known—who knew his Hebrew—to tell me the truth about Psalm 138:2. He assured me that the Hebrew is to be literally translated, "You have magnified Your word above all Your name."

To be doubly sure, I contacted my friend Rabbi Sir David Rosen, an erudite Orthodox Jew in Jerusalem. Here is what he wrote to me: "The translation should be, 'You have exalted Your word (or Your speech) above Your Name', i.e., the Divine Word is more important to Him than His Name." David added that "word" referred to the *Torah*— God's commands. Amazing.

In this book you will have seen that I take *Word* to refer to Holy Scripture—the Bible. I don't think this fundamental if not elementary point can be made too often. In other words, when I refer to Word and Spirit, I mean the Bible and the Holy Spirit. I have, therefore, made a deliberate choice in my use of *Word* in this book: I mean the Bible.

It should be noted, however, that two Greek words are translated as "word" in English—*logos* and *rhema*. Since these words are interchangeable, one must not press any hoped-for distinction too far. That said, generally speaking—and for the purpose of this book—I choose to make *logos* refer to the Word of God in *print*. I say this because *logos* also refers to the Word of God in *person*: "In the beginning was the Word...and the Word became flesh" (John 1:1, 14).

Furthermore, Paul's last word to Timothy included this command: "Preach the word [*logos*]" (2 Tim. 4:2). Could Paul have used *rhema* instead of *logos* in 2 Timothy 4:2? Yes, he could have used either. Again and again, they come to the same meaning.

The Greek word *logos* and words that spring from it are used more than three hundred times in the New Testament. *Rhema* is used at least seventy times. There have been some who wanted to show that *logos* is a stronger word—that only *logos* referred to Scripture. However, that view won't hold up. For example, when Jesus quoted Deuteronomy 8:3, "Man shall not live by bread alone, but by every *word* that comes from the mouth of God," *rhema* is used by Matthew (4:4). This alone shows that *rhema* can be used to mean Scripture as well as *logos*.

I could quote many such instances. I talked about this with Dr. Craig Keener, arguably the greatest New Testament scholar in the world today. He told me he once thought he could make a case that there is a considerable difference between *logos* and *rhema*. But he eventually realized such a case could not be made. The words are used interchangeably. This shows that one should never build one's theology on Greek! There are times when the Greek can enlighten. I use it only when I think it can be helpful. There is nothing holy about *koine* Greek, which is the kind of Greek used in the New Testament. It is what the common person spoke two thousand years ago. And yet there are times when an understanding of Greek can be helpful. As for *logos* and *rhema*, the former is more often used to denote Scripture, but *rhema* can also be used! Therefore, we must guard against making a theological case on the use of a particular Greek word.

This said, I have made a deliberate decision to treat the word *rhema* as it is *popularly* used by many sincere Christians today. Although they lack etymological support for it, they often use *rhema* to refer to a prophetic word or "word of knowledge" as in 1 Corinthians 12:8 (KJV) or "utterance of knowledge." It would probably surprise them to learn that the Greek word translated as "word" or "utterance" in this verse is *logos*, not *rhema*.

I am not going to try in this book to straighten out tens of thousands of sincere Christians by telling them they should stop using *rhema* when it could equally mean *logos*! It is not a battle worth fighting. But at the same time, I have chosen to use *logos* and *rhema* in a way that, hopefully, will be clear to you. I will put "rhema word" in quotation marks to visually represent that I am using the term the way it is popularly understood.

SERIOUS CAUTION

I urgently need to say something very important at this stage. I would say it is gravely important. Because *rhema* and *logos* can be used interchangeably, there are those who hastily conclude that a prophetic word—which they want to call "rhema word"—is equal to Scripture. Really?

I reply: Never. Never. Never. Never. Never. To do this is dangerous and will encourage people to trivialize Holy Scripture. That is what Satan wants. You should reject any prophetic person who encourages you to equate a word of knowledge from him or her as equal to infallible Scripture. If those giving you a word of prophecy have integrity, they will urge you to weigh their words carefully. They will always bow to Holy Scripture.

Regardless of the stature or reputation of the person giving it, never accept a prophetic word given to you as equal to Holy Scripture—even if the prophetic word turns out to be true. The fact that a prophetic word turns out to be true still does not give it canonical status. There are levels of authority; only Holy Scripture should be seen as the infallible Word of God.

I know a man of very high profile who says he is "too busy to read his Bible." He has a prophetic friend he consults daily, "What would the Lord have me to do today?" It is only a matter of time that this man will either come to his senses or have a huge crash that will sideline him. If any of us *uses* God only to get "a word" rather than to get to know Him for His own sake, we will sooner or later have a fall. God is no respecter of persons. He wants us to seek more *of* Him than more *from* Him. I make this point in my book *More of God* (Charisma House). God is looking for a people who want more *of* Him.

The devil does not want you to want more of God or for you to believe in the infallibility of Scripture. Satan has used liberal Bible scholars for a century or more to destroy people's faith in the Word of God. He is using some prophetic people in a rather different way today; they lure people away from trusting Holy Scripture and want you to believe their prophetic words or their words of knowledge. The devil will use liberals. He will use prophetic people. He will do whatever it takes to get you to doubt the truthfulness, faithfulness, and reliability of God's infallible Word.

You might be wondering, "Is the desire to receive a 'rhema word' good or bad?" It is good to hope for and expect what is often regarded as a "rhema word." However, I say this under the assumption that one reads his or her Bible daily because you want to know the Bible well.

I will come clean. I myself hope for and pray for a "rhema word" virtually every time I read the Bible—whether in my daily reading or when I preach. Yes, when I preach, I hope God will speak to me afresh and show me things I have not thought of before. I would define the "rhema word" I am seeking as when God's Word becomes very, very direct and very, very real; when it is unquestionably genuine and true. It can happen when I am very discouraged. It can happen when I need clear guidance. It can happen when I am routinely going through my Bible reading plan. It might happen when I least expect it.

Dr. Lloyd-Jones introduced me to the plan designed by Robert Murray M'Cheyne, a famous preacher in Dundee, Scotland. One of the thrills of my ministry was getting to preach in M'Cheyne's church in Dundee a few years ago. I had to pinch myself that I was there. I was actually given what might be called a "rhema word" following that evening service. Before I share more about that, let me start at the beginning of the story.

On my way to Dundee I received a phone call from a Scottish friend. He said, "I hear you are going to speak in M'Cheyne's pulpit tonight."

"Yes indeed," I told him. He then told me this story:

> Six months after M'Cheyne died at the age of twenty-nine, a young pastor walked several miles to visit M'Cheyne's church. He found an elder on the premises. "Tell me, sir, how can I preach like Robert Murray M'Cheyne?"
>
> The elder said, "Come with me." He took the young pastor to M'Cheyne's desk. "Sit here, put your elbows on the desk, bury your head in your hands, and let the tears flow." Then the elder said, "Come with me." He took the young pastor to M'Cheyne's pulpit. "Put your elbows on this pulpit, and your head in your hands, and let the tears flow."

After I finished preaching, I opened my Bible in M'Cheyne's old pulpit. My eyes fell directly on these words: "Streams of tears flow from my eyes" (Ps. 119:136, NIV). I wrote the date, July 15, 2007, in the margin of my Bible. M'Cheyne was known for weeping in his pulpit.[1] That was a sort of "rhema word" to me for that occasion. I took it as a confirmation from the Lord that I was in His will to be there precisely at that moment.

Although it is rare, I have had God speak to me directly and undoubtedly by opening the Bible randomly at a critical moment. I can't say it happens every day. More like once a year—if that. It is a questionable thing to do—to be fully responsible and transparently honest with you, my reader. I have been taught *not* to do this—even when greatly tempted. After all, you are—in a way—putting God on the spot. When you open your Bible, He *has* to speak—after all, it is all His Word!

You may have heard the account of a man who was severely depressed and opened his Bible for a "word." His eyes fell on the verse where Judas Iscariot hanged himself! He decided to try once more: his eyes fell on the words, "Go and do likewise." Now extremely distraught, he tried one more time: "What you do, do quickly." That is probably an apocryphal story, but it is nonetheless a valid illustration of the danger of doing this.

That said, in June 1970 at a Southern Baptist Convention, I was high up in the balcony listening to a sermon but pleading with the Lord to know the next step forward. The issue: Should I finish my education or stay where I was at the time—pastor of Lauderdale Manors Baptist Church in Fort Lauderdale, Florida? We were happy there. Nothing was wrong; all was good—except my growing frustration that I would eventually be sorry if I did not pursue further education through a seminary.

I knew that even if I gave up my church, it would take at least five years to complete what I always wanted to do—get a degree from a British university. "But," I said to myself, "I will be forty years old by then. What is more, I know the Gospel. I know my Bible. What can I learn at seminary?"

Although I tried to talk myself out of going, I felt an

underlying persuasion that I should do it *now* or regret it for the rest of my life. "How will I feel when I am forty years old? Will I be glad then that I did it? Yes. However, is this the Lord talking to me, or is it me talking to myself?"

I reached for my little New Testament I always carried with me. I had a deep-seated feeling that God was about to speak. My heart pounded as I held my New Testament in my hand. Then I prayed, "Lord, if You are going to speak, please let the word be objective—a word that stands on its own, not merely a 'Thus says the Lord, I am with you' sort of word."

I opened my New Testament, and my eyes fell on these words: "And Moses was learned in all the wisdom of the Egyptians, and was mighty in words and in deeds. And when he was full forty years old, it came into his heart to visit his brethren the children of Israel" (Acts 7:22–23, KJV). That did it for me. I turned to Louise and said, "We will resign Lauderdale Manors this Sunday. We're moving for me to finish my education."

I never looked back. That is one of the clearest words from the Lord I ever received. It answered two things that gripped me: (1) Why go to seminary when I know the Bible? Answer: Moses was learned in the wisdom of the Egyptians; it was part of his preparation. (2) The age forty was a huge factor; Moses was forty when God really began to prepare him—that is, to launch him into the primary calling or purpose for his life.

In other words, I believe that God can speak like this. He can use the Bible; He can use a person with a prophetic word.

However, I need to offer another caution. It is a real

concern of mine regarding a rather sad development. In recent years some Christians have discovered what is popularly called "rhema." There are those who *live* for what they perceive as a "rhema word." A specific word. A personal word. A quick word. A word that eliminates the need to know the Bible. It cuts out the need to apply the Scriptures to one's personal life: "Should I take this job?" "Should I marry this person?" It is a bit like people who go to McDonald's, Kentucky Fried Chicken, or Burger King because they are in a hurry. They are too busy to seek God in Scripture, to wrestle in prayer, or to wait on God.

IMMEDIATE AND DIRECT VS. MEDIATE AND INDIRECT

In my book *Holy Fire* I state that cessationists (those who believe that the gifts of the Spirit ceased long ago) hold only to a soteriological doctrine of the Spirit.

This doctrine claims that the Holy Spirit only works to *apply the preaching* of the Gospel. The word *soteriology* refers to salvation. Cessationists do not believe that the Holy Spirit can work immediately and directly in the human heart as He did in the Book of Acts. They believe the Holy Spirit gets involved in the preaching of the Gospel and applies the Word in human hearts so that people become convicted of sin, righteousness, and judgment to come. These people are, of course, right to believe that the Holy Spirit works in this way. But they are wrong to think that the Holy Spirit works *only* in this manner.

It is important for one's doctrine of assurance to know you are saved. There are two levels of assurance.

Level one: syllogistic reasoning

This level is called the indirect or mediate witness of the Holy Spirit. For example:

> All who believe in Jesus are saved.
> I believe in Jesus.
> Therefore, I am saved.

What is wrong with that kind of reasoning? Nothing. It is absolutely right. It is the Holy Spirit who applies the Gospel and leads people to trust Jesus Christ alone for their salvation. It is not that they necessarily *feel* anything; it is an intellectual process. It is cerebral. It is reasoning. The English Puritans—especially William Perkins (1558–1602)—know it as a "practical syllogism." Many if not most people come to initial assurance of salvation this way.

They are quite right to say: "I know I am saved because Jesus died for me on the cross." However, there is a higher level of assurance.

Level two: the "immediate and direct witness of the Holy Spirit"

I learned this phrase from Dr. Lloyd-Jones. The practical syllogism is not immediate and direct; it is *mediated to us by reasoning*. It is sound reasoning. It is safe and secure. But there is such a thing as an immediate and direct witness of the Spirit. It is *as though* it bypasses the mind. It is when the Holy Spirit testifies to the *heart*. It is the most amazing feeling.

What is more, this type of assurance is so powerful that one does not actually *need* reasoning to be sure that he or she is saved! The Holy Spirit Himself tells you that you are a child of God. Dr. Lloyd-Jones always called it "the highest form of assurance."

This kind of experience was typical with the original Methodists. They believed that when a person became a Christian, he or she *felt* something! They *knew* that they were born again by the direct witness of the Holy Spirit. It was a conscious experience. That is why Dr. Lloyd-Jones wanted to be called "a Calvinistic Methodist," as George Whitefield and Evan Roberts were known.

There are two points of view on this. Some believe this immediate and direct witness of the Spirit comes at conversion. That is exactly what happened in the house of Cornelius. These were unconverted people until Peter began preaching to them:

> While Peter was still saying these things, the Holy Spirit fell on all who heard the word. And the believers from among the circumcised who had come with Peter were amazed, because the gift of the Holy Spirit was poured out even on the Gentiles. For they were hearing them speaking in tongues and extolling God. Then Peter declared, "Can anyone withhold water for baptizing these people, who have received the Holy Spirit just as we have?" And he commanded them to be baptized in the name of Jesus Christ.
> —ACTS 10:44–48

This passage shows that people received the immediate and direct witness of the Spirit at conversion. It is my observation that what happened at the house of Cornelius can still happen, but I doubt it happens often.

Therefore, I believe this immediate and direct witness of the Spirit more often comes to those who have *already been converted*. It happens when people want *more* than the Holy Spirit applying the Gospel via a practical syllogism.

My friend Charles Carrin, who became a Primitive Baptist pastor, tells how he wanted more than what he experienced at conversion—real though that was. He asked his brother, "Is there not more?"

His brother replied, "No, Charles, you got it all at conversion."

Years later, having been in the ministry for a good number of years, he was invited to be a chaplain at a federal penitentiary in Atlanta and assigned to an inmate who had been miraculously converted while in prison. This prisoner also had received the immediate witness of the Spirit along with certain gifts of the Spirit. Charles was supposed to provide spiritual help, but instead, Charles began to realize that he *needed* spiritual help! After a while Charles experienced the immediate and direct witness of the Holy Spirit. His Baptist church subsequently threw him out!

Why should a person disdain the idea of wanting more? Why are some threatened by the idea of more? I suspect that when told they "got it all at conversion," some are relieved of the need to press on for more of God. They feel they can sit back, stay in their comfort zone, and refuse to be bothered by the idea that there is anything "more" after conversion.

This is not so. You and I should surely want as much of God as we can get.

The question, therefore, is: "Can I have the Spirit without

the word?" If A. W. Tozer got it right, we cannot have the Spirit without a "measure of truth." The question follows: How much truth is necessary to have the Holy Spirit? Is there a minimum threshold? In other words, what "measure" of truth does one need? I would answer: level one, syllogistic reasoning. ("I believe Jesus is the Son of God, that He died on the cross for my sins and rose from the dead; therefore, I am saved.")

Having said this, I would add that in my experience a surprising number of Charismatics who emphasize the Spirit often lack the basic assurance of salvation. I have been startled to see how many Charismatics, though they came to Christ in faith, sadly assume that their *good works* are why they will go to Heaven.

How could this be? Does it mean these people have never been converted? I would not want to go that far. Strange as it may seem, I believe there are many people who—owing partly to shallow theology taught in the pulpit—somehow forget how and why they came to Christ in the first place.

Yes, it is possible they were never converted. However, I want to be gracious and say that I believe most are converted but, owing to a superficial theology, they do not come up with the right answer to the question: "If you were to stand before God, and He were to ask you, 'Why should I let you into My Heaven?' what would you say?" In all honesty I think it is possible for some people to give the wrong answer when, in fact, they are regenerate. One reason I believe this: such people are so *quick to accept the truth when they hear it.* This tells me that they were regenerate or they would not have embraced the Gospel with their hearts when it was put to them.

This is known as *implicit faith*. It is what the woman of Samaria had. She believed in what Jesus said, and her testimony led others to affirm that Jesus was the Savior of the world (John 4:42). She testified about Him. She would not have known that the blood of Jesus Christ saves us. Implicit faith is in operation when you *believe a measure of truth you discern in your heart*. Such a person accepts more truth when they hear it, which is proof that they are regenerate.

Since I retired from Westminster Chapel, God has opened doors for me to preach in many countries of the world—to Charismatics and Evangelicals. So many—both Spirit and Word people—lack the sound basis for assurance. Those, however, who are regenerate fully accept the Gospel when they hear it.

This is why sound, solid, clear theology needs to be preached regularly from the pulpit. So often people take for granted the elementary truths of the Gospel. This is one of the reasons I wrote the book *Whatever Happened to the Gospel?*

These things said, there is such a thing as the immediate and direct witness of the Holy Spirit. It is sometimes called the "rest of faith," sometimes the "baptism of the Holy Spirit," and sometimes the "sealing of the Spirit" (Dr. Lloyd-Jones' favorite phrase). It is my observation that, more often than not, those who believe the measure of truth they have received are saved. Some lack the fullness of the Spirit; some lack a robust theology of the Word.

To refer to the main point of the previous chapter, it may

seem to be an incongruity that one could have the Spirit without the Word. However, I believe A. W. Tozer got it right. The fact is, some genuinely have the Spirit but with a *measure* of truth. I have also taken my cue from Dr. Lloyd-Jones. You will recall that he quoted John Wesley—the founder of Methodism—to uphold his own doctrine of the immediate witness of the Spirit! This is why he called himself a Calvinistic Methodist. Wesley himself was not truly Reformed in his theology, although he had a clear understanding of justification by faith. Dr. Lloyd-Jones loved to point out that Wesley even taught George Whitefield the Calvinist the doctrine of justification by faith!

Logos (the printed Word) and rhema (whether spoken or in print) may be used interchangeably. A logos Word may be a rhema word; a rhema word may be a logos Word.

These things said, I would go to the stake for my belief that it is more God-honoring to want to know Holy Scripture for its own sake than to live merely to get a "rhema word." I believe both Evangelicals and Charismatics need to heed this lesson.

Chapter Eight

THE SILENT DIVORCE

*The same day Sadducees came to him, who say that
there is no resurrection, and they asked him a question,
saying, "Teacher, Moses said, 'If a man dies having no
children, his brother must marry the widow and raise
up offspring for his brother.' Now there were seven
brothers among us. The first married and died, and
having no offspring left his wife to his brother. So too
the second and third, down to the seventh. After them
all, the woman died. In the resurrection, therefore, of
the seven, whose wife will she be? For they all had her."*

*But Jesus answered them, "You are wrong, because you
know neither the Scriptures nor the power of God. For
in the resurrection they neither marry nor are given
in marriage, but are like angels in heaven. And as for
the resurrection of the dead, have you not read what
was said to you by God: 'I am the God of Abraham,
and the God of Isaac, and the God of Jacob'? He is
not God of the dead, but of the living." And when the
crowd heard it, they were astonished at his teaching.*

—MATTHEW 22:23–33 (CF. MARK 12:18–27)

W HY BE A Christian? This question is of utmost importance. Do you have an answer? Some would say,
"You should be a Christian because you will be a happier
person." Really? The first person I baptized in London was
a Los Angeles Jewish businessman who was converted one
Sunday evening at Westminster Chapel. We later became
friends, even spent parts of holidays together. He was won-
derfully converted, but he said to me one day, "Before I
became a Christian, I was a happy man." He wasn't complaining; he was admitting that being a Christian was
costly—and sometimes painful. None of his family or his
friends became Christians.

Some might answer this question, "You should become
a Christian because it could help your marriage." Really?
Divorce rates might prove otherwise. I have found that
marriages are helped when couples put Jesus Christ first in
their lives; they are not only faithful to each other but stop
pointing the finger and mutually forgive each other for the
other's faults.

The reason a person should be a Christian, says Paul, is
because of the wrath of God (Rom. 1:18; 5:9; 1 Thess. 1:10).
Most Christians can quote John 3:16: "For God so loved
the world that he gave his one and only Son, that who-
ever believes in him shall *not perish* [meaning that they will
not go to Hell] but have eternal life" (NIV, emphasis added).
Once a person is a Christian, he or she becomes a part of
the body of Christ—the church. God wants the church to
be the salt of the earth, as I mentioned at the beginning of
this book. We become salt and light when we uphold the
Scriptures and manifest the power of God with equal force.

The last thing we want is for these two to be separated, and yet they have been.

This chapter is about a divorce between the Word and the Spirit. I believe God hates this type of divorce as much as He hates the divorce of a husband and wife (Mal 2:16, NLT; see footnote in ESV)—even more so, if that is possible.

It was a silent divorce. It is impossible to know precisely when it took place. It may have happened many times in the course of church history. Sometime before AD 65, Paul wrote of a future "rebellion" (2 Thess. 2:3). The King James Version calls it "a falling away." Between AD 90 and 100, Jesus, speaking from the right hand of God in Heaven, said that the church of Ephesus had "abandoned the love you had at first" (Rev. 2:4). What was their first love? The Gospel. Read the Book of Ephesians alongside Acts 19 and 20. The Gospel was paramount at Ephesus. So too was the evidence of power.

What is more, when you read the earliest writings of the Apostolic Fathers (people such as Ignatius and Polycarp from the second and third centuries)—as I show in *Whatever Happened to the Gospel?*—the Gospel appears to have been replaced by moralism and emphasis on good works. The Gospel is the "power of God for salvation" (Rom. 1:16). But Paul said that in the last days there would be people "having the appearance of godliness, but denying its power" (2 Tim. 3:5). That is the Word without the Spirit.

It is a gospel sometimes upheld by cerebral teaching that intentionally rejects the gifts of the Spirit. Often it is good, sound doctrine, but it lacks power. Paul calls this quenching the Spirit or putting out the Spirit's fire (1 Thess.

5:19; cf. ISV). An example of this is cessationist teaching, as I show in *Holy Fire*. Such teaching—which has utterly no foundation in Scripture—quenches the Spirit before the Spirit is allowed to manifest His power.

At the original Word and Spirit Conference in October 1992, I first expressed my view that there has been a silent divorce in the church, generally speaking, between the Word and the Spirit. When there is a divorce, sometimes the children stay with the mother; sometimes with the father. In the divorce between the Word and the Spirit, you have those on the Word side and those on the Spirit side.

WHAT IS THE DIFFERENCE?

Take for example those on the Word side. Their message is that we must:

- get back to the Bible;

- earnestly contend for the faith once delivered to the saints (Jude 3);

- get back to Reformation doctrine (justification by faith as taught by Martin Luther);

- rediscover assurance of salvation as taught by John Calvin; and

- return to the teaching of the sovereignty of God as preached by Jonathan Edwards.

What is wrong with this emphasis? Nothing, in my opinion; it is exactly right.

Take those on the Spirit side. Their message is that we

must get back to the Book of Acts where there were signs, wonders, and miracles—gifts of the Spirit in operation. When they had a prayer meeting the place was "shaken" (Acts 4:31). Get into Peter's "shadow," and you were healed (Acts 5:15); lie to the Holy Spirit and you were struck dead on the spot (Acts 5:1–10).

What is wrong with this emphasis? Nothing, in my opinion; it is exactly right.

The problem is that neither will learn from the other; they talk past each other and don't take the other point of view seriously.

THEN AND NOW

According to Jesus in Matthew 22:29, the Sadducees were ignorant of two things: the Scriptures and the power of God. Remember, the Scriptures refer to the Bible (the Word); the power of God, to the Holy Spirit (the Spirit).

In the case of the Sadducees, they had only the Old Testament scriptures, of course. Jesus was saying they were ignorant of the Old Testament. We have the New Testament, which they did not have. Never forget that the New Testament is as infallible and God-breathed as the Old Testament. They have equal status as the Word of God. When I mention the *Word* or *Scriptures*, I am referring to both the Old *and* New Testaments.

A difference between the situation in Jesus' day and now is probably this: whereas the Sadducees were ignorant of *both* the Word and the Spirit, I suspect that a vast segment of the church today is often ignorant of one or the other— or the emphasis is on one or the other. You have those who are knowledgeable of the Word. I call them Word people. You have those who emphasize the Holy Spirit or are knowledgeable of the gifts of the Spirit. I refer to them as Spirit people.

In my experience Word people resent it if someone says they are ignorant of the Holy Spirit. They are indignant. "Whatever do you mean? We believe in the Father, the Son, and the Holy Spirit!" I don't mean to be unfair, but I have sometimes wondered if their true conviction is "God the Father, God the Son, and *God the Holy Bible*," as Jack Taylor often puts it.

Likewise Spirit people feel insulted if someone says they are ignorant of the Word—or at least good theology. "We believe in the Bible! That is all we preach!" they will say with fervor. To suggest they don't have much interest in sound theology puts their backs up. They don't get it.

This is why we have the two camps today. Like a divorced couple, they talk past each other, never really listening to each other since each group is totally convinced that they don't have a problem.

Hence the problem continues. The church is asleep. The world is going to Hell, and we don't seem to care all that much. We all want to stay in our comfort zones.

SOME SAD DEVELOPMENTS IN BOTH WORD AND SPIRIT CAMPS

There are developments since the 1992 Word and Spirit Conference that I must discuss, although both maladies have been in existence for longer than that.

Charismatic shifts

1. Prosperity teaching

The common denominator that held most Charismatics and Pentecostals together in early years was an emphasis on signs, wonders, miracles, and the gifts of the Spirit—mostly healing. However, that is not true in some Charismatic or Pentecostal ministries today where the emphasis has shifted to prosperity teaching.

Here is partly how it happened. There was an undoubted anointing of healing and miracles in the 1950s. People were truly healed—of cancer, polio (before the Salk vaccine became widely used), and immobility. People in large numbers got out of wheelchairs, and either carried their wheelchairs home or threw them away. In the meantime some of the high-profile people who emphasized healing—and who saw people healed—began television broadcasts. The money flowed. But for some reason healings started to wane. With fewer genuine miracles, one needed another reason to keep people watching and keep the money flowing.

Around this time, the emphasis switched from healing miracles to financial miracles. Nowadays a TV personality seldom finishes a show without mentioning finances and giving the implication that God does not want you to be poor. I am not saying there is no biblical basis for some of this teaching. I have written a book called *Tithing*, and in it I stress that "you cannot outgive the Lord."[1] However, I fear some have gone too far in their emphasis.

My friend Rev. Kenny Borthwick, a Church of Scotland minister and unashamed Charismatic, told me that he often watches religious television through the eyes of unsaved people. After watching for hours, he turned to his wife and said, "If I did not know otherwise, I would say that Christianity is all about money."

What is more, I fear that many prosperity teachers have, sadly, given sincere and sound Charismatics a bad name. I know many Charismatics, and I do not wish to paint with too broad a brush and say that all Charismatics are focused on prosperity. Still, there is no denying that we only find this unhealthy emphasis among Charismatic ministries.

2. Faith healers

Sadly, some who prayed for the sick became known for three things. First, they kept people in wheelchairs away from the front of the auditorium where they would have more hope of receiving prayer. One famous faith healer refused to pray for people in wheelchairs.[2] Second, they began blaming people who needed healing for their lack of faith if they were not healed, giving people with sickness or disability a guilt trip. This sort of thing did not characterize the era of healing anointing that was around decades ago. Third, a spirit of arrogance seems to have emerged in some when it comes to one's own faith. For example, one famous preacher said, "If the apostle Paul had my faith, he would not have had his thorn in the flesh."[3] This kind of teaching is wrong, and many sincere people who don't know solid theology are carried along by it.

Evangelical shifts

1. Avoiding the Spirit

I will not enter much further into the cessationist issue. I have dealt with that in *Holy Fire*. It is my observation however that evangelical ministers generally who are not cessationists might as well be. They keep a safe distance away from anyone who might cause a stir. They fear losing members or getting involved with anything that might hurt their finances. They remain in their comfort zones. They often seem terrified at any current activity of the Holy Spirit. Moreover, I will repeat what I have said many times—that if it were not for the gift of speaking in tongues, there would probably be no objection to the gifts of the Spirit. True revival never comes in a neat and tidy package.

2. Avoiding serious issues

I am disturbed at how rarely anyone opposes Freemasonry. There are Southern Baptists—pastors and laymen—in high places who are Masons. Many, many deacons and lay leaders in different denominations in America are Masons, and hardly anyone says a word.

I also must mention the lack of preaching on eternal punishment in most pulpits today. I'm afraid this would include a growing number of Charismatic churches too. Those who have chosen to believe in *annihilationism*—the view that people come to nothing as being the meaning of eternal punishment—have increased dramatically. Also, many of those who reject annihilationism seldom emphasize that the lost will go into conscious eternal punishment after they die.

To summarize: as the church in Ephesus had left their first love, the Gospel, so too do many who believe the Gospel in their heads but who do not preach it with passion. Soul winning is never popular.

Furthermore, most people today have never heard of the word *propitiation*—the heart of the Gospel. It means that Jesus' shed blood turned God's wrath away. The justice of God was *satisfied* by the death of His Son. For people to be saved, they need only to transfer their trust from good works to Christ's shed blood.

THE SADDUCEES

Let us consider how this relates to the passage I quoted at the beginning of this chapter. In Matthew 22, when the Sadducees came to Jesus with their biases and prejudices, Jesus said to them, "You are in error because you do not know the Scriptures or the power of God" (v. 29, NIV).

When the crowds heard the way that Jesus expounded the Old Testament, they were *"astonished* at his teaching" (Matt. 22:33, emphasis added). I am fascinated that Jesus' teaching could bring about such an emotion. They were dazzled by His teaching. It is the same Greek word used in Matthew 7:28–29 when, at the end of the Sermon on the Mount, the crowds were *"astonished* at his teaching, for he was teaching them as one who had authority, and not as their scribes." It is the same word used in Luke 9:43 when Jesus cast out a demon; everyone was "astonished."

I often think of the Graham Kendrick song "Restore O Lord." It talks about God restoring the honor of His name. How do you suppose the restoration of that honor is to come about? Some might say that it will only come through a demonstration of signs, wonders, and miracles. That could be true. However, I believe that God is going to withhold the phenomena of signs and wonders from the church generally until two things coalesce: the Scriptures and the power of God—the Word and the Spirit.

I refer again to where the apostle Paul said, "Our gospel came to you not simply with words but also with power, with the Holy Spirit and with deep conviction" (1 Thess. 1:5, NIV). Paul said to the Corinthians: "My message and my preaching were not with wise and persuasive words, but with a demonstration of the Spirit's power" (1 Cor. 2:4, NIV). Paul consistently combined the Scriptures with a demonstration of the power of God: the Word of God and the Spirit of God. Another way of putting it, as we shall in more detail later, is that the Word and the name of God will be remarried.

But Jesus' way of putting it in Matthew 22:29 is the combination of the Scriptures and the power of God. The word for *power* is the same as the word used in Luke 24:49 when Jesus said, "Stay in the city until you are clothed with power from on high." It's the word used in Acts 1:8: "You will receive power when the Holy Spirit has come upon you." The two together—the Scriptures and the power of God—are the only explanation for what happened when Peter preached on the day of Pentecost. It was a force that defied a natural explanation. Only God could do it.

To avoid being like the Sadducees in Jesus' day, we ought to know two things they didn't know: the Scriptures *and* the power of God. Both must be emphasized and experienced simultaneously.

The Sadducees mainly descended from priestly families. They traced their ancestry back to the priest Zadok, from whom their name derives. They were the aristocracy of the day, fewer in number than the Pharisees but far more influential. The Sadducees didn't *think*—they *knew;* they were the experts on the Law of Moses.

The Sadducees had minimal respect for the prophetic. Their authority was the Pentateuch, the first five books of the Bible. To them, the prophets of the Old Testament were second-class—whether it be the canonical prophets (those who have a book named after them, such as Isaiah or Ezekiel) or the Elijahs or Elishas of Scripture. According to Acts 23:8, the Sadducees' main doctrinal distinctions were: (1) no resurrection of the body; (2) no angels; and (3) no such thing as disembodied spirits—they felt that the soul died with the body. They were annihilationists.

The Sadducees despised Jesus of Nazareth. It didn't matter to them that the Pharisees felt the same way about Jesus. They were determined to prove that their doctrinal distinctions were correct and that Jesus was a quickly passing phenomenon.

In the dialogue between Jesus and the Sadducees in Matthew 22:23–32, the Sadducees were very proud of themselves for coming up with an airtight case that would prove their point and put Jesus in His place. "'Teacher,' they said, 'Moses told us that if a man dies without having children, his brother must marry the widow and raise up offspring for him'" (NIV). They followed this legal statement with an illustration. They made it up. It was theoretically possible, but in any case, it suited their purpose. "There were seven brothers among us. The first one married and died, and since he had no children, he left his wife to his brother. The same thing happened to the second and third brother, right on down to the seventh. Finally, the woman died. Now then, at the resurrection, whose wife will she be of the seven, since all of them were married to her?" (NIV).

Jesus was not intimidated by their attempt to ensnare Him. His reply was, "You are in error" (NIV). I once heard William Hendriksen (1900–1982) state it this way: "You are deceived." In a word: "You are ignorant."

What a thing to say to those who thought they knew everything! How many of us have enough honesty, integrity, and objectivity about ourselves to see and admit when we have been deceived? The response I'm describing requires a teachable spirit, the antithesis of the Sadducees' temperament. In this case their deception and unteachable spirit sprang from ignorance.

Jesus said, "You do not know." Jesus is not using the Greek word *diaginōskō*, which is often used to show what has been revealed. That's the way some people know things: by revelation. He uses another Greek word, *oida*, which often means knowledge of a well-known fact. Jesus is virtually saying, "You're ignorant; you're not even acquainted with that for which you think you're an expert."

Imagine that! Jesus was telling the *experts* in the Pentateuch, "You are *ignorant* of the Scriptures." Could you imagine saying that to a seminary professor, Oxford don, or New Testament scholar?

Then Jesus added, "You're not only ignorant of the Scriptures, but you are also equally ignorant of God's power." Now, why bring that up? They weren't the slightest bit interested in that subject. They had not come to talk about God's power; that was the furthest thing from their minds. It was Jesus who brought it up. Nothing was more irrelevant to them.

I wonder how many Christians today are like that. You have felt that your knowledge of Scripture was enough, that your emphasis upon doctrine was enough. You think that Scripture is all that matters, and talk of God's power was for the apostolic era only.

PHARAOHS WHO "KNOW NOT JOSEPH"

I will say it again. The church today, generally speaking, is like the ancient pharaoh "who did not know Joseph" (Exod. 1:8). Joseph, prime minister of Egypt, had made the children of Israel heroes in Egypt. The fat of the land was theirs. The pharaoh of that time gave them everything they wanted, but that pharaoh died. In the meantime the children of Israel grew and multiplied. The new pharaoh felt threatened by the growing number of Israelites, and he did not care about Joseph, who had also died. The new pharaoh persecuted the children of Israel. It was as though Joseph never existed.

The church today is filled with millions of pharaohs "who did not know Joseph." There are those who aspire to do God's work but don't know His Word. I referred earlier to John Wimber. I heard him teach at Royal Albert Hall in London that Luther and Calvin gave us the Word in the sixteenth century, but this is the twentieth century, and God wants us to do the "works."

Later that week I shared my heart with him as lovingly as I knew how, "John, you are teaching 'pharaohs that knew not Joseph.' You are assuming that the people of the twentieth century have the Word because the Reformers gave us the Word four hundred years ago. Many who are trying to do the works today don't really know the Word."

He laid down his knife and fork, put both forefingers on his chest, and said, "You have touched the very vortex of my thinking right now. I accept what you have said." I felt he meant it, but I never knew if he tried to apply it.

The truth is, we are a generation of pharaohs—both as the church and the Western world—who seem to know nothing about or owe nothing to our historical past.

THE HOLY SPIRIT AND OUR MEMORY

In John 14:26 Jesus said the Holy Spirit would bring to our remembrance what we had been taught. When you read that verse, don't forget that Jesus' disciples had been trained. They were taught by Jesus Himself; they'd heard a lot and learned a lot. Would they forget what they had learned? "Don't worry about that," Jesus said. "The Holy Spirit will bring to your minds what you learned."

I hear people talk about the desire to be Spirit-filled, and I applaud that desire. However, I have to tell you that if you are empty-headed before you are Spirit-filled, you will be empty-headed after you are Spirit-filled. The Spirit cannot remind you of something you never knew in the first place.

I believe that revival is coming—an unprecedented outpouring unlike anything our generation has seen. The question is, Are we ready for it? Have we been trained? Have we been taught? The people God will use most are those who have sought His face (getting to know Him and desiring more *of* Him) rather than His hand (what they can get *from* Him). He is looking for a people who have searched His Word and stood in awe of it.

Job could say, "I have treasured the words of his mouth more than my daily bread" (Job 23:12, NIV). The psalmist could say, "I have hidden your word in my heart that I might not sin against you" (Ps. 119:11, NIV). How many of us memorize Scripture—an art that has virtually perished from the earth? You ask, "What's the use? Why read the Bible? Why memorize Scripture? Why endure teaching? It is so boring; it is so uninspiring."

I answer, "One day it will pay off; the Spirit will bring to your mind what you've learned."

THE WORD AND THE NAME

This unprecedented awakening, which I believe is coming, will come when the Scriptures and the power of God come together. Another way of putting it, as I said earlier, is that the Word and the name of God are rejoined—remarried. The two ways God unveiled Himself in the Old Testament were through His Word and His name. "I bow down toward your holy temple and give thanks to your name for your steadfast love and your faithfulness, for you have exalted above all things your name and your word" (Ps. 138:2). The King James Version got it right, as I keep saying; it reads, "Thou hast magnified thy word above all thy name."

What is the Word? It came to Abraham, Isaac, and Jacob. Abraham believed it and was saved. "Abram believed the LORD, and he credited it to him as righteousness" (Gen.

15:6, NIV). People are still saved this way, but what does it say? "'The word is near you, in your mouth and in your heart,' (that is, the word of faith that we proclaim); because, if you confess with your mouth that Jesus is Lord and believe in your heart that God raised him from the dead, you will be saved" (Rom. 10:8–9).

What about the name? It was first disclosed to Moses. It says in Exodus 3:6—the very verse that Jesus quotes to the Sadducees, "'I am the God of your father, the God of Abraham, the God of Isaac and the God of Jacob.' And Moses hid his face, for he was afraid to look at God." However, read Exodus 6:2–3: "God also said to Moses, 'I am the LORD. I appeared to Abraham, to Isaac and to Jacob as God Almighty, but by my name the LORD I did not make myself known to them'" (NIV).

How could this be? Abraham, Isaac, and Jacob knew and responded to the Word of God, but they did not know His name. How is it possible? Because God's Word has priority over His name. Hearing the Word saves us. That is how God made Himself known to Abraham. That's how Abraham was saved; that's how we are saved.

This explains how it is possible for a church to continue without signs and wonders. Signs and wonders do not save us. We're saved by the Gospel that tells us Jesus died on the cross for our sins and rose from the dead. Hearing that Word of grace and embracing it by faith is what saves us. This is why we will go to Heaven when we die and not to Hell. The blood that Jesus shed on the cross two thousand years ago is the most precious commodity in the history of humanity. The blood that dripped from His hands, feet, and head cried out to God, and it satisfied the justice of God. By it we are saved; without it we are lost. It is hearing that Word that brings us from death to life.

People can see signs and wonders and go to Hell. People can experience signs and wonders and go to Hell. People can minister signs and wonders and go to Hell. Jesus said, "Many will say to me on that day, 'Lord, Lord, did we not prophesy in your name and in your name drive out demons and in your name perform many miracles?' Then [Jesus] will tell them plainly, 'I never knew you. Away from me, you evildoers!'" (Matt. 7:22–23, NIV).

I sometimes cannot help but wonder how a verse like that makes some faith healers and prophetic people feel.

That said, remember that it is also possible to know the Word and be lost. It is possible to be sound in doctrine and never be converted. Some people sit under the ministry of preaching, and you discover to your astonishment that they have never been converted. So don't say that just because you're sound in doctrine, you're going to Heaven. You can be sound in doctrine and be lost. The devil believes and trembles (Jas. 2:19).

I know of at least two different people—an elderly deacon and a highly respected physician—who had attended Westminster Chapel for years but who, according to them, came to the assurance of salvation late in life. One of them, having sat under my ministry for years, admitted he had not been genuinely converted until he took the Evangelism Explosion course as taught by the late D. James Kennedy (1930–2007). I was surprised to discover this. However, it goes to show that a person can sit under a theologically sound ministry—and enjoy biblical preaching and teaching—without themselves converting or having the assurance that they are saved. I should add that neither of these people lacked good works or holy living. Indeed, they were exemplary—to the hilt. But for some reason the truth that we are saved by "faith alone plus nothing" had not touched their hearts.[4] It is, after all, something that can be revealed only by the Holy Spirit. That said, I suspect that both of them had, as I stated above, implicit faith.

Make no mistake: the Gospel of Jesus Christ is complete without signs and wonders. However, the Bible is not complete without signs and wonders.

One day God appeared to Moses. Moses got up that morning not knowing that day would be different. He was watching sheep at the foot of Mount Horeb and saw a bush on fire. Perhaps there was nothing unusual about that; maybe he'd seen it before. But he noticed something different this time: the bush didn't burn up. One of two things would be true. Either the bush was different, or the fire was different. He began to look more closely.

Many want what Moses wanted. He wanted a rational explanation for what was happening. We all have our questions. Some things are too deep to be revealed this side of eternity. God said simply, "Stop. Take off your shoes. You are on holy ground." (See Exodus 3:5.) In that event, an event through which Moses would never again be the same, God unveiled His name—"I AM WHO I AM" (Exod. 3:14). He went on to say that He revealed Himself to Abraham, Isaac, and Jacob as God Almighty, but He didn't reveal His name to them.

Unprecedented phenomena accompanied the unveiling of God's name—signs and wonders. It began with the burning bush. It continued with Aaron's rod, which was turned into a serpent, and with the ten plagues of Egypt, culminating with the night of Passover and the crossing of the Red Sea on dry ground. An unprecedented kind of power inaugurated the revelation of God's name. Signs and wonders defied a natural explanation.

How do we summarize the relationship between His Word and His name? The Word relates to God's integrity: His promise, His grace, His inability to tell a lie. It is the way we are saved. His name refers to His honor: His reputation, His power, and His influence.

So while God's Word refers to His integrity, His name refers to His vindication.

However, the Sadducees knew about neither. "You are in error," said Jesus, "because you do not know the Scriptures or the power of God" (Matt. 22:29, NIV). *They didn't even know what Exodus 3:6 really meant*—that the issue behind that verse was the honor of God. Whatever *happened* to Abraham, Isaac, and Jacob? Were they just relics of the past? Did they die like dogs or cattle or trees?

Jesus gave the Sadducees the shock of their lives. He turned their smug interpretation on its heels, and with it not only affirmed the resurrection of the dead but of angels and immortality of the soul as well. The existence of an intermediate state demands the resurrection of the body. He said to them in Matthew 22:30, "At the resurrection people will neither marry nor be given in marriage; they will be like the angels in heaven" (NIV). *Resurrection* means the end of death. There will be no need for the procreation of the race. We will be like the angels in Heaven.

At this point Jesus said, as it were, "Oh, by the way, about the resurrection of the dead, have you not read what God said to you, 'I am the God of Abraham, the God of Isaac, and the God of Jacob'? He is not the God of the dead but of the living." In other words, Abraham, Isaac, and Jacob are alive and well. They are in Heaven right now with the angels. Their souls and their disembodied spirits are with the Lord at this moment, worshipping Him.

FOUR WAYS TO RECEIVE POWER

These verses contain the basis for power—power in the right sense. At the natural level, and often in the wrong sense, we all want power. This is why people want a pay raise. This is why people want a promotion. In 1960 John F. Kennedy (1917–1963) was asked, "Why do you want to be president?" He said, "Because that's where the power is."[5]

In a spiritual dimension, we should be greedy for power. Jesus said, "Stay in the city until you are clothed with power from on high.... You will receive power when the Holy Spirit has come on you" (Luke 24:49; Acts 1:8). As we have seen, the apostle Paul warned us against "having a form of godliness but denying its power" (2 Tim. 3:5, NIV).

What then is the basis for God's giving spiritual power to His followers? I identify four aspects.

1. Personal reading of the Scriptures

It is almost humorous to read what Jesus said to the Sadducees: "As for the resurrection of the dead, have you not *read*?" (Matt. 22:31, emphasis added). Nevertheless, we have to ask ourselves a question: "Have I read my Bible? Have I read it completely through?" There are those who have no Bible reading plan, no plans even to have a plan. Jesus would say to you, "You don't know the Scriptures."

If you are a church leader or have been a Christian a good while, would you be ashamed for people to know how much you read your Bible or pray? Different polls over the years have shown that very few Christians spend daily time with the Lord. And we wonder why the church is power-less! Martin Luther prayed three hours a day. John Wesley prayed two hours a day. Where are the Martin Luthers today? Where are the John Wesleys?

A strong personal prayer life and reading of the Scriptures daily are the first steps to Holy Spirit power.

2. Personal revelation of the Scriptures

Notice how Jesus put it. "Have you not read what God said to *you*?" (Matt. 22:31, emphasis added). In other words, Jesus said, "It's for you, Sadducees."

However, if it was available to the Sadducees, it is available for anybody. If it could be true for the skeptical, sure, smug Sadducees, it is true for anybody. God originally said it to Moses, but Jesus said, "It's for you." What is "it"? It is personal revelation when God's Word gets hold of you.

Are you interested in receiving a prophetic word? Then I ask: When is the last time the Scriptures got hold of you and shook revelation knowledge into your life? If a text gets hold of you, chances are you've got hold of it. When is the last time that God's Spirit went right through to your heart like a laser beam when you were reading your Bible?

3. Personal rethinking of the Scriptures

You perhaps know the familiar words of Exodus 3:6; they became almost a cliché: "I am...the God of Abraham, the God of Isaac and the God of Jacob." These words were as well known to the Sadducees as a verse like John 3:16—the Bible in a nutshell—is to most of us.

Jesus said, "Have you not read Exodus 3:6?" How would you feel if somebody said to you, "Have you not read John 3:16?" You might say, "You're not serious!"

You can hear the biting sarcasm in Jesus' words: "Have you not read what God said to you?" Of course, you couldn't have told the Sadducees anything about Exodus 3:6. That verse to them was like the ABCs. To them, it merely meant, "We worship the same God in our day as they worshipped in their day." Jesus was virtually saying, "Wrong. You missed the real meaning altogether. What it means is that Abraham, Isaac, and Jacob are *alive*. God is not the God of the dead but of the living."

The Sadducees were devastated and humiliated.

Many of us lock ourselves in to a point of view concerning certain Bible verses or teaching, just like the Sadducees. Some of us think we know it all. We have accepted a hand-me-down point of view with no questions asked. We have secondhand Bible revelation and doctrine. "So-and-so believes it; I believe it. It was taught to me this way, and therefore, I've always believed it."

There is often no personal rethinking by which we acquire the real meaning of any verse. It comes by emptying ourselves before the Lord. Come to Him with openness, saying to Him, "Lord, is it possible I have it wrong when it comes to understanding this verse—or this point of view?"

4. Personal release of the Spirit

For many of us this is the hardest thing of all to do. It means giving up any "claim" upon God—a feeling of entitlement, as if He owes us something. This is a major step of faith.

For some it might seem unbecoming to talk about releasing the Most High, releasing the Holy Spirit, or setting God free, but it is true. We bind the Spirit by holding on to our fear or remaining in our comfort zone. We release the Spirit not only by totally forgiving every single person on earth but by stepping out in faith to do what He has commanded.

Moses had to do that. He had to lift that rod! The Lord said to Moses:

> Why do you cry to me? Tell the people of Israel to go forward. Lift up your staff, and stretch out your hand over the sea and divide it, that the people of Israel may go through the sea on dry ground.
> —EXODUS 14:15–16

Simply put, releasing the Spirit is having the courage to do what God tells you to do. You will know in your heart of hearts what He is putting to you. I had to invite Arthur Blessitt to Westminster Chapel. I had to go to the streets of Buckingham Gate and Victoria personally and talk to passersby about Jesus Christ. I knew I would pay a price, but it was worth it. I had to be willing to sing choruses and modern songs in worship—an unprecedented procedure for us in Westminster Chapel. On June 6, 1982, I had to give my first invitation at the end of a sermon to call people forward to confess their faith—a practice never done in Westminster Chapel before.

Incongruous though it may seem, when I set the Holy Spirit free, I too was set free. Also, it is interesting to me that my first sermon on the life of Joseph—which became my book *God Meant It for Good* (MorningStar Publications)—was when I gave the first appeal for people to walk forward to confess Christ openly. Dr. Lloyd-Jones never did this. He reasoned that one might usurp the work of the Holy Spirit if one pressured people to come forward—as some evangelists actually did and still do. But I never did this and never will.

I wrote a book *Stand Up and Be Counted* (Zondervan)—my outline for giving an appeal without pressuring people and honoring the Spirit and not usurping Him. In fact, when Dr. Lloyd-Jones would preach for me at my little church in Lower Heyford, Oxfordshire, I *always* gave an appeal after his sermon. He said to me verbatim: "The way you do that I have no problem with at all." I gave people an opportunity to do what they *want* to do, not what they don't want to do. But it still took courage to do it! This is an example of releasing the Spirit.

However, we also release the Spirit when we pursue both the fruit and gifts of the Spirit with equal earnestness; when we stop quenching the Spirit by our fear, biases, and stubbornness; and when we let God be God. We release the Spirit when we become willing to forgive those who have hurt us in any way (Eph. 4:30–32). Holding a grudge binds the Spirit; total forgiveness sets Him free. It may be surprising how being devoid of bitterness eradicates so many prejudices.

The release of the Spirit comes from the Spirit Himself. It is what He does, and the proof that He has done it is that you even feel free! Where the Spirit of the Lord is, there is freedom and liberty (2 Cor. 3:17).

As I discussed in chapter 2, the question to ask is, How are you going to get on good terms with the Spirit? If we want power, it's going to have to come from the Spirit. If we are going to get on good terms with the Spirit, then we have to get on good terms with His book—His greatest product. We honor Him when we show that we love His Word—so much so that we want to know the Bible backward and forward.

Do you say that you love the Holy Spirit? He's asking you today, "Do you really?" A release of the Spirit will result in a personal renewal of power that will restore the honor of God's name.

Forgive me if I'm wrong, but I suspect that when it comes to the theme *Word and Spirit*, Evangelicals seem to be more interested in the Word than they are the Holy Spirit. Charismatics seem to be more interested in the Holy Spirit than they are the Word. It is my view that we must love both equally, pursue both equally, and emphasize both equally.

I fear that some have so little confidence in the authority of the Word that it has hardly crossed their minds how the Word of God can astonish. As we saw earlier, Jesus could astonish people with the Word as easily as He could with signs and wonders. You might say, "Well, if only I could have Jesus teaching me personally all the time, I too would be astonished."

I answer: You have the greatest expositor with you. He is in you: the Holy Spirit. We will release the Spirit to the degree that we (1) stand in awe of His Word, (2) stop quenching the Spirit by unbelief, and (3) stop grieving the Spirit by bitterness and unforgiveness.

The scope for power, therefore, will be found to the degree that we value His own Word. Signs following will be His seal on us. Power that flows from His name will be in proportion to our love for His Word. When we express that love, don't be surprised to see healings, miracles, signs, and wonders take place even during the preaching of the Gospel. There may be no need for people to get into prayer lines. It can happen right where the people are.

My father named me after his favorite preacher, Dr. R. T. Williams (1883–1946), who used to say to young preachers: "Honor the blood and honor the Holy Ghost." By that he meant that the Gospel should emphasize Jesus' blood and that the Holy Spirit should be in control of the services we lead. We must never upstage the Gospel, but we must be open to the Spirit.

I, therefore, fear that a silent divorce has taken place between the Word and the Spirit, between the Word and the name, between the Scriptures and the power of God.

In our day there are those whose sole emphasis is the Word. Others say, "I want to see power." There are those who come to our services expecting to hear the Word. At Westminster Chapel I used to hear, "Thank you for your word." That is what they came for; that was what they got. Others want to see a demonstration of power. They want to see things happen.

When these two—the Word and the power of the Spirit—are brought back together, a remarriage will occur. The simultaneous combination will create a spontaneous combustion. The day will come when those who come to see will hear, and those who come to hear will see.

PART III:
THE NEXT GREAT
MOVE OF GOD

Chapter Nine

WHERE PROMISES AND POWER MEET

Our gospel came to you not only in word, but also in power and in the Holy Spirit.

—1 THESSALONIANS 1:5

I BORROWED THIS CHAPTER's title from a line in Graham Kendrick's song "Jesus, Restore to Us Again," first sung at the Word and Spirit Conference in 1992. It feels thrilling to think of a place where promises (the Word) and power (the Spirit) meet, but how does it work? What is the point of the Word and Spirit coming together? What difference does it make? In this chapter I will endeavor to answer these questions as I describe to the best of my ability what it will look like when the Word and the Spirit come together.

FIVE LEVELS OF THE WORD AND SPIRIT COALESCING

First, I believe there are five levels of the Word and Spirit coming together.

Level one: believing it

Let's face it. We either accept this, or we don't. We believe it is a valid concept, or we don't. Some would say that a separation between the Word and Spirit is a false dichotomy; the Word and Spirit never separate. If one takes the view that the Word and Spirit always flow together and there is no such thing as a separation—or divorce—between the Word and Spirit, then this book is false and therefore irrelevant. If that is what you believe, then this book has no chance of impacting you, much less changing your life. So the first question is: Is what I have written in this book true or false?

Level two: emphasizing it

There are those who believe what I have written. They think it is a good word, a timely word. Not only that, one should stress from time to time that the notion of bringing the Word and Spirit together is a good idea. We should see it as an ideal match, namely, for the Word and Spirit to come together.

At this, then, there are those who nod their heads positively. Some might even say, "We need more of this emphasis," but it is always out there as a *future* thing to anticipate or pray about, like kicking the can down the road. In the meantime we have other important things to think about, and nothing ever happens. It is perhaps like those who are not cessationists but who have no worries whether the Word and Spirit ever coalesce simultaneously.

Level three: trying it

At Westminster Chapel we began healing services by praying for the sick in connection with the Lord's Supper. Then we moved to praying for the sick every Sunday evening following the preaching. Our deacons acted as elders. Those who wanted the anointing of oil called for the elders of the church (Jas. 5:14) by sitting on the front rows of the church. We did this for the last few years I was at Westminster. We saw genuine healings—not a lot, but some. It was absolutely worth doing,, not only for the healings but also because it brought everyone closer to one another.

We were doing our best to give the Holy Spirit an opportunity to work. My part was preaching the Word. Likewise, we were open to the Spirit by offering the anointing of oil. There is more, however. The entire congregation that remained following the preaching would be in an attitude of prayer. Anyone who did not want to pray or be prayed for was asked to go home or go to the back hall for coffee. This meant that all in the main auditorium were inviting the Holy Spirit to manifest in any way He was pleased to do. A great sense of the presence of God became a regular occurrence for my final days at the chapel.

Level four: tasting it

To refer to our practice at Westminster, God indeed gave us a taste, but it was only a *taste*—just enough to make one want more. We saw unquestioned healings and at least one deliverance (a man who did not have a full night's sleep for twenty-five years owing to demonic interference was set free). There were others we would hear about later.

The revival I prayed for never came to Westminster Chapel. Following the visit of Arthur Blessitt in 1982, our Pilot Light ministry brought a huge upheaval for a while— the worst trial of my whole life. But on the other hand, there was an anointing that settled on the chapel that stayed throughout my time there—a sweet presence, great unity, peace, joy, and easy preaching. All of it was a taste of the Word and Spirit coalescing.

Level five: experiencing the fullness of power

Fullness of power means true revival, which we never had at Westminster Chapel, but it is what I pray for daily— that "Isaac" will come. (I'll explain more about this in chapter 11.) It will be a move of the Holy Spirit that even exceeds the Great Awakening in New England, the Cane

Ridge Revival, the Wesleyan Revival in England, and the Welsh Revival. I don't know where it will begin—possibly in London—but it will be a worldwide phenomenon. As one prophetic person put it: "a resurgence of the fear of the Lord is coming." It will fall "suddenly, unexpectedly, and unannounced." It will not be an "encore"; it will be unprecedented. He added that "it will be a waste of time telling people to get ready. It will just come."

I hope he is right. I believe he is right. It is what I live for and long for more than anything in the world. Smith Wigglesworth prophesied it just before he died. It will signal the end of the silent divorce between the Word and Spirit.

THE WORD AND SPIRIT AND PREACHING

I have chosen to write the next several paragraphs in the context of preaching, but I believe Christians in any vocation can apply these principles to their lives. Please do not skip over this section if you are not a minister by trade; all of us are called to share the Gospel with the lost around us. You may never stand behind a pulpit, but you can reach people with the Gospel that your pastor will never reach. My prayer is that God uses this teaching to ignite the personal ministry of any Christian.

Experimental preaching is my term for anointed preaching. No one has improved upon Phillip Brooks' (1835–1893) definition of *preaching*, which he gave in his historic Yale lectures. He defined *preaching* as "the bringing of truth through personality."[1] I would define *experimental preaching* as "releasing the Holy Spirit to be Himself." I regard preaching as an experiment, a test of whether or not the Holy Spirit *can get past me*.

Following Aristotle, experimental preaching assumes a thesis or major premise, then a minor premise, or hypothesis, and then a conclusion. My thesis is:

- Major premise: the Holy Spirit wants to be Himself to the people I address.

- Minor premise: I am the instrument of the Holy Spirit.

- Conclusion: the Spirit becomes Himself to those I address.

Experimental preaching is what our fathers called unction. Oddly enough, the words *unction* and *anointing* are used very few times in the New Testament, and the meaning does not fit with what is generally referred to as "preaching with unction." Unction, or anointing, comes from the Greek word *chrisma*—not *charisma*, which comes from a different root. *Chrisma* means anointed.[2] The root word is *chrio*, from which we get the name Christ, meaning anointed one.[3] There are other Greek words, such as *parresia*, which means boldness or freedom, or even various forms of *logos*, which often better express what our fathers called "unction"—thus Paul expressed the wish that he would be given "utterance"—*logos*—in Ephesians 6:19.

AN UNUSUAL GREEK WORD

There is an unusual Greek word used only in the Book of Acts. The Greek word *apophtheggomai* is translated three different ways, depending on the tense: "utterance" (2:4); "addressed" (2:14), and "speaking" (26:25).[4] Because of this it is almost impossible to give the exact meaning, but one thing is clear: it refers to speaking aloud, possibly with a raised voice.

I would not want to push this point too far, but it is noteworthy to me that the same Greek word, *apophtheggomai*, is used for (1) the ability to speak in tongues (Acts 2:4)—which is supernatural; (2) Peter's preaching on the day of Pentecost (v. 14)—when he received the highest possible level of unction; and (3) Paul addressing King Agrippa (26:25)—a very important moment in Paul's ministry. I cannot be sure why Luke chose this word, but it is interesting that he uses it to refer to these three extraordinary events. The implication is that what enabled the disciples to speak in tongues is what enabled Peter to preach as he did and Paul to speak to Agrippa as he did. In other words, all three events refer to unusual power.

To put it another way, what the 120 disciples in the Upper Room could do only as the Spirit enabled them on the day of Pentecost—utter words in other languages—is what Peter did as he preached in his *own* language on the day of Pentecost. In order for Peter to speak powerfully in his own language, he had to have the same power that enabled the 120 to speak miraculously in other languages. Peter spoke in his own language, but he possessed the same ability to utter the words. Paul no doubt spoke in his own language to Agrippa, but Luke uses this word for what required unusual help.

We are talking about very unusual power, a kind of power I have personally experienced (perhaps) only twice, but power that can be present when the Spirit is released to be Himself.

Many of the Greek words mentioned in these lines at first appear very similar. Some are; some aren't. For example, *charisma* and *chrisma* sound alike and look very much alike, but they come from different root words. I would add that the Greek word *chrisma* is a valid word for experimental preaching (1 John 2:20, 27). It comes from *chriō*, which refers to the act of smearing as with an ointment,[5] similar to when the psalmist referred to the "precious oil poured on the head...running down on Aaron's beard" (Ps. 133:2).

Chrisma is not the same thing as *charismata*, which means grace-gift. It doesn't even come from the same Greek word. But sadly today it seems that people are more interested in *charismata* or *charisma* than in the self-effacing quality inherent in the *chrisma* anointing.

Right now we need this anointing upon our preaching above all else. In my view unction or anointing alone will open new vistas to make truly great preaching a reality. Were this dimension to be recovered by the modern pulpit, it would do more to restore public respect for the church and the Christian faith than anything else I know.

My thesis, then, is that the Holy Spirit wants to be Himself and reach those I address unhindered, ungrieved, unquenched, and undisguised. It lies within my power to hinder or release the Spirit. The question is, Will I block the Spirit or let Him get past me?

A famous story about John Calvin (1509–1564) and Martin Luther illustrates my meaning. There's no proof that Calvin ever met Luther face to face, but he did regard Luther as a father in the faith. Calvin wrote a letter to Luther making some suggestions to Luther on the doctrine of the Lord's Supper. I wish that Luther had received Calvin's letter; Luther needed what Calvin had to say about it. But Philip Melanchthon (1497–1560), who was at Luther's side, rightly or wrongly intercepted the letter, read it, and never let Luther see it, regarding it as too sensitive for the aging Luther to read.[6]

Now we too can do that sort of thing with those we address. We may be afraid to let our hearers experience what the Spirit would be and do. We may block the Spirit from being Himself because we fear their reaction.

Vince Lombardi (1913–1970), who was the greatest coach American football history has ever seen, was asked his secret to winning so many football games. He replied, "Winning isn't everything; it's the only thing."[7] I share that same sentiment regarding the anointing. It should be what we want more than anything and what we aspire to more than any goal we can conceive. It cannot be something we seek *some* of the time; it must be something we pursue *all* of the time, every minute of every day.

It is why and how Paul could say that his message came with the Spirit's power (1 Cor. 2:4) and that the Gospel he preached came not simply with words but with power and the Holy Spirit (1 Thess. 1:5).

Paul also said, and this bothers me, that he wanted to preach "without using the language of human wisdom, in order to make sure that Christ's death on the cross is not robbed of its power" (1 Cor. 1:17, GNT). The reason this bothers me is because I have been guilty too often of using words "with human wisdom"—such as when I use an acrostic or alliteration in a sermon.

Would I not be right in saying that this kind of preaching is something exceedingly rare today? For all I know, it is something that cannot be transmitted by the printed page or through audio or video recordings. I never will forget the first time I looked at George Whitefield's sermons; I read one page, found very little substance, and thought, "Oh, well, it's Whitefield; I'll try another page." I kept reading, finished the sermon, and thought, "What on earth is this?" I read the other sermons, and I couldn't believe it. They were breathtakingly simple.

The same is undoubtedly true of John Sung (1901–1944), the man who saw a great revival in China during the 1920s and 1930s. I met a man who was converted under Sung, and he would talk to me about him, describing his sermons and their impact. I longed for the day when I could read some of Sung's sermons. Finally I got a copy; they seemed utterly devoid of substantial content.

Dr. Lloyd-Jones loved to tell the story of an American couple who crossed the Atlantic some two hundred years ago, hoping to hear Whitefield preach at his Tabernacle on Tottenham Court Road, London. The couple said they had a very rough crossing. They came into Southampton very tired, but they inquired whether George Whitefield would be in his pulpit on Sunday. Word came that he would be there, so the next day, still tired from their journey, they sat in the Tabernacle with great expectation.

They said that when he stood, he too appeared tired. They thought perhaps he'd been very busy and hadn't had time to prepare. At first his sermon seemed very rambling, and they thought, "What have we done, coming all the way here for this?"

But during the sermon, something indescribable happened and the atmosphere became heavenly. Afterward the couple said they would have crossed a thousand seas to be there. They left the Tabernacle *physically* refreshed from the journey. Reportedly someone went up to Whitefield and asked for permission to print his sermon. Whitefield replied, "Yes—if you can get in the thunder and the lightning."

As I said, I believe perhaps twice in my ministry I experienced a touch of this power. The first was on a Sunday evening in Bimini, Bahamas, when I preached for Rev. Sam Ellis (1919–2003), known as Bonefish Sam, the famous fishing guide. That morning I had preached for Dr. D. James Kennedy at the Coral Ridge Presbyterian Church in Fort Lauderdale, Florida. I flew to Bimini that same afternoon to preach in the small church with nineteen people present. That morning I had preached in Kennedy's gown; that evening, in short sleeves and tennis shoes.

In Bimini, as we all knelt to pray, I asked the Lord what I should speak on. Hebrews 13:8 came to me: "Jesus Christ is the same yesterday and today and forever." The presence of God was suddenly as real to me as when I was baptized with the Spirit on October 31, 1955. The person of Jesus was so real.

I spoke to the Bahamians on how Jesus is the same even in His appearance—He still has the print of nails in His hands. I had very unusual power for this little group—unlike I had ever experienced. I asked the Lord, "Why didn't You give me this power this morning at Coral Ridge with movers and shakers of America present? Why don't You give me this at Westminster Chapel?"

I don't know the answer. I only know God did it for nineteen Bahamians who will probably never turn the world upside down.

At Westminster Chapel it happened only one time in twenty-five years. When preaching on Philippians 1:12, "What has happened to me has really served to advance the gospel," lo and behold, God gave me unusual insight and power. When I sat down afterward, there was a feeling of awe on all present. Wow. I had always longed for a touch of the anointing, and for once I had it. I will never forget it as long as I live.

Dr. Lloyd-Jones called this unction an "access of power." It is "God acting." I remind you of my thesis: the Holy Spirit wants to be Himself to the people I address. "The spirit indeed is willing, but the flesh is weak" (Matt. 26:41), and yet I am the instrument of the Spirit; I stand between God and men either to intercept or to transmit what the Spirit wants to be and to do. If I do not block the Spirit, He will be Himself to my hearers.

HOW DO I BLOCK THE SPIRIT?

Human wisdom

The Spirit can be blocked by words of human wisdom. This is one of my greatest temptations, especially when nearly everything I utter publicly is recorded and will sometimes be in print. So the temptation for me is to write a book rather than preach a sermon. This encourages a lop-sided emphasis on the correct use of words.

The apostle Paul was one of the greatest intellectuals in the history of the world, one of the greatest rhetoricians of all time. If anybody could speak with the "wisdom of words," it was he. If you don't believe that, read 1 Corinthians 13. However, if Paul made any effort at all, it was in being careful *not to speak* in such a manner that would call attention to the well-turned phrase rather than call attention to the cross. The great Charles Spurgeon used to say, "Labor to be plain."[8]

There are three rules here:

1. Don't try to be eloquent.

2. Don't try to be eloquent.

3. Don't try to be eloquent!

Perverting the text

We block the Spirit if we don't allow the true meaning of the text to flow unhindered. The anointed preacher should be like a transparent windowpane that calls no attention to itself, but it enables others to see right through it. When we distort the text, we're like cracked windows or, worse,

153

stained-glass windows that are never intended to be seen through.

We can mishandle a text three ways: first, by treating a verse contrary to its context; second, by importing an idea, however valid, that the text did not call for; third, by superimposing our own idea upon the text.

The Spirit wrote the text, and the Spirit knows what it means. My duty is to discover the meaning of the text, not to sound clever or to import an idea or superimpose my opinion onto the text. The text must speak for itself.

Copying others

I block the Holy Spirit when I am not myself or when I try to imitate someone else. We tend so often to suppose that there is a quality in another that we think is not in ourselves. We see it in another person and pick up his mannerisms. We think, "I'm going to be like that, and everyone's going to think I'm like him."

There was a memorable preacher years ago in Texas who was unusually powerful. He had a powerful anointing on him, but when he got going—nobody knew why he did this—his left hand would come up over his ear. He'd just keep on preaching. They made that man professor of preaching at Southwestern Baptist Theological Seminary in Fort Worth, Texas. You could always tell one of his students! When those young men thought they were "ringing the bell," that left hand would go up over the ear!

I told that story at Southwestern Baptist Theological Seminary, hoping to pull the story out of the woodwork. It worked. An old professor came up to me right after the service. He said, "I know exactly who you mean."

I said, "Well, would you please tell me why that left hand would go over his left ear?"

He said, "It's very simple. He was hard of hearing, and he could hear himself better when he spoke like that." But those young men didn't know that. They were simply imitating a weird habit, thinking it was part of the anointing!

Dr. Lloyd-Jones told a similar story. He said, "There was a man in South Wales who had an eccentric habit. When he preached, his hair would get down in his eyes. He wouldn't take his hand and push it back; he would shake it back. Sure enough, young preachers all over South Wales began shaking their heads when they were preaching." Lloyd-Jones added that one of the preachers who began shaking his head was bald!

It is the hardest thing in the world for some of us to come to terms with our own personality. I had to admit a long time ago that I am no Martyn Lloyd-Jones—to accept myself and risk what people will think if I am myself. Why? Because I have come to see that I block the Spirit when I am not myself. God made me the way I am; He made you the way you are—He threw the mold away when He created you.

We need to learn this. We dignify Him when we accept ourselves. When you learn to like yourself, God likes that. He looks down and says, "Well, I'm glad you like yourself—you know, I made you that way." We, therefore, affirm Him when we accept ourselves as we are.

Avoiding difficult scriptures

We block the Holy Spirit by not following through with the obvious meaning of the text and its implications. I suspect that some preachers don't like to preach through a book in the Bible or through a chapter verse by verse because they're afraid to face up to a verse that they know will be coming up. They may not know what the verse means, or they may be afraid to discuss what it means, so they jump around the Scriptures instead. Sometimes it takes courage to pass on the plain meaning of the text to the hearers. We may think that it will rob us of a chance to be eloquent, but to do otherwise will rob them of the simple truth that all our hearers have a right to hear.

Back in 1979 I felt led to preach through the Book of James. But I hesitated to do so because I did not understand James 2:14: "What good is it, my brothers, if someone says he has faith but does not have works? Can that faith save him?" I knew the traditional view—that we are saved by faith alone—but saving faith is never alone; there will always be works to prove that one is saved. I did not think that was what James meant. But what *did* James mean? I believe the Holy Spirit prompted me that if I started at James 1:1, I would know what James 2:14 meant when I came to it.

And that is what happened! I share this story in more detail in *Whatever Happened to the Gospel?* When I arrived at James 2:14 in the series, the meaning opened up: it is not talking about assurance of salvation but the effect that works have on others, especially poor people. In actual fact, the *him* in James 2:14 (accusative, masculine, singular) refers to the *poor man* in James 2:6 (accusative, masculine, singular). I shared this first with Dr. Lloyd-Jones. He looked at me and said, "You convinced me." Dr. Michael Eaton wrote me a year later to say it not only convinced him but led him to open the door of his church in Johannesburg to people of all color.

All preachers want to master a text, but great preachers are mastered *by* the text. When the text masters us, we will state plainly what the text is saying and follow through with the application that the Holy Spirit dictates—even if that preaching gets close to the bone and threatens our lifestyle.

This brings me to my next point. Often we will not preach on a subject because we know there is something in our lives that will be obvious, and we dare not preach on it. I am convinced that many preachers will not preach on tithing because *they* are not tithers. Many preachers do not preach on witnessing because *they* don't do it. Therefore, when it comes to certain verses, we don't like to preach that which will expose our hearts. That is why the Spirit doesn't get through us.

The Reformers accused Rome of keeping the Bible from the common people, but we do the same thing if we don't pass on the obvious meaning of the text.

Personal feelings

I block the Spirit when I let a personal concern or emotional involvement get in the way of my preaching. This is sometimes called preaching *at* the people, which will never do. There are five options available to the preacher:

1. Preaching *for* the people. That's performance.

2. Preaching *at* the people. That's lack of self-control.

3. Preaching *down* to people. That's arrogance.

4. Preaching *up* to people. That's fear.

5. But there is a transaction that takes place between the throne of grace and the pew when we preach *to* the people. That is our calling.

Preaching *at* the people blocks the Spirit and leaves the people oppressed; it is always counterproductive. I know because I've done it. The temptation is to set the record straight. It is a melancholy enterprise called "self-vindication." It is assuming that the pulpit is my personal platform. James S. Stewart (1896–1990), in his book *Heralds of God*, quoted Bernard Manning: "The pulpit is no more the minister's than the communion table is his."[9]

Grieving the Spirit

I block the Spirit when I do not allow the ungrieved Spirit to master my mind in preparation and control my feelings in the act of preaching.

The Holy Spirit is a very sensitive person—in fact the most sensitive person that ever was. We often say of a sensitive person, "You'd better watch what you say around him or her." We see sensitivity as a defect in another person, calling that person hypersensitive. But the Holy Spirit is very like that! It is alarming that we rarely know, at the time, that we are grieving the Spirit. We don't feel a thing. When Samson gave his secret to Delilah, he didn't feel a thing: "He did not know that the LORD had left him" (Judg. 16:20).

158

Peter said, "Husbands, in the same way be considerate as you live with your wives...so that nothing will hinder your prayers" (1 Pet. 3:7, NIV). I know what it's like to quarrel with my wife. I know too what it's like to have my prayers hindered.

Once on a Saturday morning when Louise and I got into an argument, I slammed the door in anger, went to my desk, got out my pen, and said, "Holy Spirit, now help me to write this sermon I've got to preach tomorrow." I just sat there. It was awful. I was too proud to apologize. Our temper often *gets* us into trouble; pride *keeps* us in trouble.

I seethed for seven hours, getting not one thought for my sermon. When I finally apologized and returned to the same desk, the same Bible, and the same blank sheet of paper, ideas began to pour into my mind so quickly that I could not write fast enough. I got all I needed in forty-five minutes. It just goes to show that we can accomplish more in five minutes when the Spirit comes down than we can in five years when we try to work something up in our strength.

I block the Spirit, therefore, when I do not let the Spirit master my mind in preparation. When I'm angry, when I'm holding a grudge, when I have not totally forgiven the person who has hurt me deeply, then I have grieved the Spirit. Grieving the Spirit results in the inability to think clearly and hear from God. At least this is so with me.

Bitterness always seems right at the time. When we say something about another person that reduces his credibility, we often don't feel a thing. But later when we try to do something that we thought we were able to do, we find it's happening in our own strength—like Samson—and it's useless.

Sometimes I define *spirituality* as "closing the time gap between sin and repentance." In other words, how long does it take you to admit you were wrong? For some it takes years; for some seconds; and for most of us it's somewhere in between. If you know the way the Spirit can be grieved, often you can catch yourself and narrow the time gap to seconds so that there's no discontinuity with the ungrieved Spirit resident in you.

When the Spirit is Himself in me, He is ungrieved and therefore can master my mind. When this is the case, my preparation is a sheer delight; thoughts come—original insights I could never have thought of—because the Holy Spirit wrote the Bible, and He knows what it means.

Trying to control the Spirit in delivery

I block the Spirit when I do not let Him master my delivery. In other words, I must have the courage to pass on what the ungrieved Spirit gave me in preparation. I must refuse to let any personal concerns come between my congregation and me when I preach. It can also mean I must be willing to depart from my prepared notes and, if necessary, ruin my sermon.

One of the most memorable services of my life was when the visiting evangelist at my old church in Ashland, Kentucky, did not preach at all. It had been a memorable week. Sermon after sermon, night after night, the preacher had unusual power. I was only a teenager but could not wait for each sermon. On the closing Sunday night the place was packed. When the man stood up to preach, tears filled his eyes. I wondered, "What will he preach on tonight?" He began singing the chorus of "Wonderful, Jesus Is to Me."

I knew this chorus well. When he finished singing it, he repeated it. I thought, "When is he going to preach?" Lo and behold, he sang this chorus through for the third time! Suddenly people got up out of their seats by the dozens and came to the front to kneel and pray. The visiting evangelist never preached that night, but what a service! This man preferred to "honor the Holy Ghost," as we saw above. Rather than preach his sermon, he let the Holy Spirit take control.

Like the ointment on Aaron's beard, it may be sticky and alter my appearance or injure my pride. It is the same with a sermon or message one has prepared. Do you realize how ornate and beautiful the robe of the high priest was? Psalm 133 talks about the ointment poured on Aaron's head, flowing down on Aaron's beard and upon his robe, soiling it. I am, sadly, not very willing to do that to one of my carefully prepared sermons! But in the end this dimension can be the true experiment, testing whether the Spirit can be Himself to those I address.

I have seldom done what the previously mentioned evangelist did—sacrifice a sermon to let the Spirit take over. But that can only happen when a high level of power is already present—as it was that night.

Experimental preaching will include all three of the elements Aristotle refers to in his work, *Rhetoric*:

- *ethos*—the credibility of the speaker

- *pathos*—the appeal to the senses, when done with integrity

- *logos*—the reason or logic of the message[10]

Some sermons today are devoid of logos and long on pathos. Some are strong on logos—correctness of doctrine—but without any pathos. When the Holy Spirit is released to be Himself, we will have not only the needed balance but also the satisfaction that those we address will hear a word from beyond that defies a natural explanation.

I pray and long for the day when the silent divorce between the Word and the Spirit comes to an end and there is a mutual reconciliation and a glorious remarriage. With God all things are possible.

Chapter Ten

PROPHETIC
RESPONSIBILITY

*I say to everyone among you not to think of himself more
highly than he ought to think, but to think with sober
judgment, each according to the measure of faith that God
has assigned... if prophecy, in proportion to our faith.*

—ROMANS 12:3, 6

Do not take an oath at all.

—MATTHEW 5:34

I BECAME AWARE OF "the prophetic," as it is known in some places today, late in my ministry. Until around 1990 I would have regarded anything prophetic to refer to eschatology—the doctrine of last things. I took an interest in biblical prophecy in my teens—partly because my Nazarene pastor in Ashland, Kentucky, spoke a lot from the Book of Revelation.

By the time I went to Trevecca Nazarene University in 1953, I had it all figured out! I even taught the Book of Revelation there when the professor said, "Next week we will treat the Book of Revelation. Is there anyone here who understands it?" My hand shot up like a rocket. "Brother Kendall, would you like to teach it?"

Without hesitation I replied, "Yes." And so I did—with confidence, arrogance, and total absence of humility. I blush to think of the effect it had on the students there. Let us say that it did not endear me to them—or to the professor who graciously stepped aside to listen to my ignorance.

As I write this book some sixty years later, two things are true. First, I admit to knowing little if anything for sure regarding the Book of Revelation. Second, I have become acquainted with the most talked about prophetic person since William Branham (1909–1965). I would add that I am not sure if I understand the "prophetic" any more than I do the Book of Revelation. It is shrouded in mystery. I say that because I thought I understood it, but I now realize it is a case of history repeating itself. As I knew little about the Book of Revelation but thought I knew a lot, so too I thought I understood the prophetic but realize I know so little.

In 1991 Bishop David Pytches came out with his book *Some Say It Thundered* (Thomas Nelson)—an examination of what he called "the Kansas City prophets." The book featured four men I had never heard of but have since gotten to know fairly well. In fact two of them became close friends to my family and me. One of them, Bob Jones (1930–2014), came with Ricky Skaggs to my bedside the day following my open-heart surgery. He prophesied to me for an hour. Still being affected by the anesthetic, I barely remember all he said. The only thing I remember is that he kept referring to me as a "canopy."

I can tell you that I have been immersed in the good, the bad, and the ugly. I know enough to affirm that God can speak today in the same way He spoke to Elijah, but I also know enough to realize that the best of men are men at best. I am better off to know what I know, but I must also say that I know enough to make any honest inquirer almost disillusioned.

You might ask, Why deal with this at all? My answer: because it is so relevant.

The late John Paul Jackson (1950–2015), one of the four men referred to as the "Kansas City prophets," became a close friend. He had a lot of influence on me, and I on him. I introduced bonefishing to him and took him to Bimini, Bahamas, three times. I won't go into all his prophetic words to me, but I will mention one.

During a meal in Key Largo, Florida, he changed the subject and suddenly said to me, "R. T., you will live to a ripe old age, but if you don't get in shape physically, you won't be around to enjoy it" (or words to that effect).

I said to him many times after that, "John Paul, if none of your words to me come true, I will treasure that word about physical exercise more than all the others." I have no doubt that if he had not said those timely words, I would not be able to travel the world as I do. His words changed my life for the better. I have watched my weight ever since, do daily exercises, try to do at least twenty push-ups a day, and try to walk a mile on the treadmill in twenty minutes, and I found a godly trainer to assist me.

That said, John Paul thought he and I would have a ministry together. The day before he died, he was talking about his future. He genuinely thought he would be healed of cancer. Sadly, neither of these things came to pass.

This is partly what I mean by the prophetic being shrouded in mystery. I don't claim to understand it, but I know enough not to be overly critical. After all, the apostle Paul said, "Do not despise prophecies, but test everything; hold fast what is good" (1 Thess. 5:20–21).

"The Lord told me." "Thus saith the Lord." "God is saying." Many prophetic people utter these phrases virtually all the time. I think they should stop it. I have said this to nearly all of them that I have met. Few listen.

Many of us claim to speak for God these days, but how many of us really do speak for God? Many people claim to have a prophetic gift and give words introduced by "the Lord told me…" Countless others would not appear to be prophetic but nonetheless claim they hear directly from the Lord. Perhaps they do.

I do believe that God speaks directly to people today. To maintain the premise that God speaks directly to people is not *violating* Scripture; it is *upholding* it. As Dr. Lloyd-Jones said again and again—not only to me but also to the Westminster group he used to address every month, "God did not give us the Bible to replace the miraculous, the direct witness of the Spirit, or fresh revelation; it was given to correct abuses."

Jesus Christ is the same yesterday, today, and forever (Heb. 13:8). The Holy Spirit is the same yesterday, today, and forever. God the Holy Spirit may speak directly today—but never something that either adds to Scripture or contradicts Scripture. Let us look at the verse before and after Hebrews 13:8 to give it context:

> Remember your leaders, those who spoke to you the word of God. Consider the outcome of their way of life, and imitate their faith. Jesus Christ is the same yesterday and today and forever. Do not be led away by diverse and strange teachings, for it is good for the heart to be strengthened by grace, not by foods, which have not benefited those devoted to them.
> —HEBREWS 13:7–9

Verse 8 was written in the context of affirming that leaders spoke the word of God (v. 7) and a warning not to be led away "by diverse and strange teachings" (v. 9). Any prophetic word from God will uphold or coalesce with Holy Scripture. It will never contradict Scripture.

Neither will a direct word add to Scripture. Consider these three biblical examples.

First example

> Now an angel of the Lord said to Philip, "Rise
> and go toward the south to the road that goes
> down from Jerusalem to Gaza."...And the Spirit
> said to Philip, "Go over and join this chariot." So
> Philip ran to him.
>
> —ACTS 8:26, 29–30

God can do this today. It does not add to Scripture when
this happens. It affirms it—just as it did a little further in
verse 30 when Philip found the Ethiopian eunuch reading
Isaiah. The direct word from God will always affirm the
infallible Word of God—Holy Scripture.

Second example

> Now in these days prophets came down from
> Jerusalem to Antioch. And one of them named
> Agabus stood up and foretold by the Spirit that
> there would be a great famine over all the world
> (this took place in the days of Claudius).
>
> —ACTS 11:27–28

God can do this also today. It does not add to Scripture
in the least; it affirms that God is the living God and acts
in the here and now, not merely in the olden days.

Third example

> Let those of us who are mature think this way,
> and if in anything you think otherwise, God will
> reveal that also to you.
>
> —PHILIPPIANS 3:15

Am I to believe that Paul's words do not apply to me? Never. It shows that God can talk to me. Why would God give us the New Testament—and words such as we have in Philippians 3:15—if He cannot reveal His clear correction today? The answer is: God may speak this way today— namely, to sort us out in a manner where we know we are not only not being deceived but know He has a way of keeping us on the straight and narrow road!

Speaking personally, I live to hear directly from God. I will take any word from Him I can get—if indeed it is from Him. But I want to know it is from *Him*. I have been given enough prophetic words—from strangers and friends—to last a lifetime. I have learned not to dismiss them but to be polite. I have learned not to take them too seriously but put their words on the back burner and wait for their fulfillment.

A woman in Scotland—whom I had not seen before, nor have I seen since—rushed toward me with a word of caution, "I keep seeing your heart. It's your heart. Your physical heart. You need to pay attention to your heart and get it checked." I nodded as kindly as I could but did not take her seriously. I remembered her words a few months later when a cardiologist told me that I had aortic stenosis and would need open-heart surgery—immediately.

God might be pleased to send a prophetic word via Scripture, by another person's insights, a hymn, or even an audible voice. Yes, an audible voice; I have experienced this a few times. Not that you could hear it if you were in the same room, but clearly audible to me. However, I live mostly for insight—thoughts and interpretations of God's

Word that I've never seen before. I am in my highest realm of ecstasy when this happens.

Several questions come to mind: How much are we to share with others when we think we hear from God? Are we to claim, "the Lord told me," when we have an impression we feel is from the Holy Spirit? How many of these words or feelings are really from the Lord? Should it bother us that so many words do not come to pass which were prefaced by "the Lord told me"? What do you suppose God in Heaven thinks of all this?

When a word that was introduced by "the Lord told me" does not come to pass, obviously something has gone wrong. It dishonors the name of the Lord. It brings discredit upon the gift of prophecy.

Should we not apologize if we get it wrong? Surely if *the Lord* says something, it is going to be exactly right. Is it an encouragement when a prophetic person with a solid reputation says, "The Lord told me to tell you this"? Certainly, but what are we to believe if that word does not come to pass? I've had the "best" get it wrong in their words to me. Does it mean that the person who made the claim is a false prophet? Not necessarily.

As we just saw above, Luke portrays Agabus as a true prophet in Acts 11:28, and yet objective scrutiny of Agabus' word in Acts 21:11 will lead you to ask, "Is that really what happened?" Most people probably don't check the facts. Look at Agabus' prophecy and the details of what happened. Did Agabus get it right? Not really. Does that mean Agabus was a false prophet? No. However, Agabus said, "The Holy Spirit says." Did He? The subsequent events were not exactly the way Agabus predicted. Luke simply states what Agabus says.

Saying "the Lord told me" is a habit prophetic people find hard to break.

PERSONAL CONFESSION

I will come clean. Although I do not claim to have a prophetic gift, I have made this mistake a thousand times, e.g., saying, "The Lord told me," "the Lord gave me this sermon," and so on. There have been times it may truly have been from the Lord, and yet to say, "the Lord gave me this sermon"—even if He did—does not mean that every word in it is like Scripture!

I stopped saying, "The Lord told me," a long time ago—especially when I began to understand Jesus' instructions never to take an oath.

As you read on, I will attempt to explain why one should not say, "The Lord told me." He or she may feel it is from the Lord, but there is no need to add, "The Lord told me." I urge: do not claim that all you feel is from the Lord. You can always say, "I think I am supposed to share this with you." This way, we do no harm.

SIX LEVELS OF PROPHECY

Prophecy—if it is true prophecy—is a word directly from God unfiltered by human embellishment whether it pertains to the past, present, or future. But not all prophecy is of the same caliber. There are levels of prophecy—as in a pyramid, starting from the bottom and working to the top.

6. General exhortation (encouragement)

Dr. Michael Eaton called this "low-level prophecy." Paul encouraged this kind of prophecy (1 Cor. 14:1ff); he was not motivating someone to become another Elijah. Someone may have a "word"—whether from a hymn, dream, or even a vision—but such a word needs to be tested. As I said above, we are not to despise such prophesying (1 Thess. 5:19–20), but all words need testing.

5. Specific warnings

Certain disciples urged Paul not to go on to Jerusalem. Luke sides with them; he says that they warned Paul "through the Spirit" (Acts 21:4). Agabus similarly warned Paul, saying "the Holy Spirit says" (Acts 21:11, NIV), and yet Paul refused to heed their warning. Who got it right? Was Paul wrong to ignore them? Agabus may have been wrong; Paul may have been wrong. In any case, it did not seem to bother Paul; he went to Jerusalem anyhow.

4. Prophetic preaching

As we saw earlier, Peter said one should speak as if their words were the "very words of God" (1 Pet. 4:11, NIV). I wish this were the case in my own preaching. My basic style is expository and pastoral, but nothing thrills me more than when someone says to me, "How did you know I was there today? That is exactly what I needed." Expository preaching can be prophetic without the preacher being conscious of this. Even if he is conscious of the Lord's enabling, he should be humble about it and not say, "Thus says the Lord." I will say more about this later.

3. When forced to testify during persecution

Jesus said, "When they arrest you, do not worry about what to say or how to say it. At that time you will be given what to say, for it will not be you speaking, but the Spirit of your Father speaking through you" (Matt. 10:19–20, NIV). In the autumn of 1963, when I was pastor of a small church in Carlisle, Ohio, I was called before a group of ministers to answer charges that came from some of my church members. On the morning of my heresy trial, I supernaturally received Matthew 10:19–20 from the Lord. I felt His help that evening when answering a "heretical" charge that I claimed Jesus is God. I pleaded guilty to that charge! Those present assured me that I won the day. God gave me the exact words to say. It was the first time I needed to lean on Jesus' promise in Matthew 10:19–20.

2. Noncanonical prophecy

Nathan, Gad, Elijah, and Elisha are examples of noncanonical prophets. Could there be prophets of this magnitude and stature today? I believe so. Then can they say, "The Lord told me"? I reply: they should be the wariest of all in saying things such as "the Lord says." Why? They will be watched and examined with the most painful scrutiny. If they will keep the name of the Lord out of it and simply say something like, "I feel I must say this to you," they will maintain their integrity, credibility, and anointing. Many a modern prophet could be saved incalculable embarrassment had they been more modest in their claims.

You lose *nothing* by keeping the name of the Lord out of the picture. You embarrass the angels when you include the name of the Lord and get it wrong. As I will try to show further below, there is no need to bring in the name of the Lord when passing a caution or encouragement to someone.

1. Holy Scripture

This includes all of the Old Testament—with the canonical prophets—and all of the New Testament. Scripture is God's final revelation. No one will ever have the authority to speak like this. If any man or woman claims to speak on the same level as Holy Scripture, he or she is utterly out of order and will be found out sooner or later. Only the Bible is infallible.

LIMITS OF PROPHECY

There are several scriptures most relevant here. First, remember that each of us has but a "measure of faith" (Rom. 12:3). This means there is a limit to our faith. Only Jesus had a perfect faith because He alone had the Holy Spirit without limit (John 3:34).

Second, for those who prophesy, it must be done in two ways: (1) in "proportion" to their faith (Rom. 12:6), not going beyond the anointing, and (2) according to the analogy of faith. The Greek word translated "proportion" is *analogia*.[1] This means comparing scripture with scripture, making sure you are within the bounds of sound theology!

Third, remember that prophecies will cease (1 Cor. 13:8–9). This means there are seasons of the prophetic. The word of the Lord was "rare" at one time in ancient Israel (1 Sam. 3:1). Amos spoke of a famine of hearing the word of the Lord (Amos 8:11).

This means that sometimes God chooses to say nothing. God may choose not to speak for a generation. If so, how foolish to pretend to speak for Him. Rare is that prophetic person who will refuse to be drawn out to give a "word" when there is not clearly such a word! A common mistake of many prophetic people is that they have some form of "spiritual experience" and get a genuine word from God but then embellish it with personal exhortation or theological teaching based on their own experience to justify the spin, which may or may not be from God.

Fourth, Paul said that we know in part and we prophesy in part (1 Cor. 13:9). This means nobody knows everything and no prophet has unlimited knowledge. That should keep all those with an undoubted prophetic gift humble!

PROTOCOL OR GUIDELINES OF PROPHECY

There are certain principles we must follow to maintain transparent integrity regarding the prophetic. First, don't go beyond what you are given. This is much the same thing as Paul instructing the Corinthians "not to go beyond what is written" (1 Cor. 4:6). So too with a prophetic word; do not embellish it. I have known more than a few prophetic people who receive an undoubted word from the Lord but end up messing it up by embellishing it.

Second, be very, very careful to honor the name of the Lord. I come now to the most sobering and delicate part of this chapter. What I share now is already in print in two places: see my treatment of Matthew 5:33–37 in *Sermon on the Mount* (Chosen Books) and my exposition of James 5:12 in *The Way of Wisdom* (Paternoster Press).

Here is what is stated in James 5:12: "But above all, my

brothers, do not swear, either by heaven or by earth or by any other oath, but let your 'yes' be yes and 'no' be no, so that you may not fall under condemnation." This warning is addressed to poor Christians who had been mistreated by well-to-do Christians, as pointed out in James 5:1–6. The temptation for both was to claim "God is on our side" by bringing in God's name. James' word: do not do that. Do not abuse that name by claiming God is with you and not them. Hence, "Do not swear," that is, do not claim to have God on your side—whether you are poor or well-to-do. Do not say, "I swear by the name of God that He is with us—not you." In other words, says James, leave God's name out of it. Quit using His name to make yourselves look good.

This is why a prophetic person should be careful not to say, "Thus says the Lord" or "The Lord told me." Why? Because you are claiming to have inside knowledge that God has spoken through you—using God's name to make yourself look good. When we do that, we are not trying to make *God* look good; we are trying to make ourselves look good. This breaks the third commandment that says we must not misuse the name of the Lord (Exod. 20:7). It is taking God's name in vain when you *use* His name to puff up your prophetic utterance.

We must therefore honor the third commandment in the Mosaic Law (the Ten Commandments): "You shall not take the name of the LORD your God in vain" (Exod. 20:7). The New International Version says, "You shall not misuse the name of the LORD your God."

In the Sermon on the Mount, Jesus gave His interpretation

of the Law in three instances: (1) regarding the sixth commandment (murder); (2) regarding the seventh commandment (adultery); and (3) regarding the third commandment on the name of the Lord. This is in Matthew 5:33–37. James therefore quoted Jesus in James 5:12: "Above all, my brothers, do not swear, either by heaven or by earth or by any other oath, but let your 'yes' be yes and your 'no,' be no, so you may not fall under condemnation." Here James particularly addressed those workers in the field who had been mistreated by wealthy believers. The temptation for poor laborers in the fields was to say, "God is on our side and against you." James thunders a warning against taking sides and using God's name. It is the worst form of name-dropping, that is, using God's name to make yourself look good.

Misusing God's name is when you bring Him into your conversation to elevate your own credibility. You are thinking of yourself, not Him. Perhaps you want people to think you are spiritual. You want to seem close to God.

I have done this too often over the years—I am ashamed to say. I have (I hope) stopped it. I believe I am to share this with everybody in these last days. Did the *Lord* tell me to share this? You tell me!

The issue here is the oath. One of the greatest privileges Christians can have is for God to swear an oath to you and me the same way He did to Abraham. The oath is seen when God grants the highest level of faith; this is what lay behind the miraculous in the Bible. If granted, the oath from God to us may pertain to (1) assurance of salvation (Heb. 4:10; 10:22); (2) advanced notice of answered prayer

(Mark 11:24; 1 John 5:15); (3) knowing you have it right theologically (Col. 2:2); (4) the prayer of faith for healing (Jas. 5:15); and (5) a prophetic word (1 Pet. 4:11).

All prophecy must be done in proportion to our faith; it is only when the oath is given to us that we know for certain we have been given a word from God. This is what lay behind Elijah's authority. As I show in *These Are the Days of Elijah* (Chosen Books), Elijah had authority before Ahab because of God's oath to him. Only when God swears an oath to you can you have the kind of authority that Elijah had before Ahab. Elijah did not bite his nails for several years wondering if he saw a cloud in the sky. He calmly said to the king, "It won't rain unless I say so." How could Elijah be so sure? "As the LORD, the God of Israel, lives, before whom I stand, there shall be neither dew nor rain these years, except by my word" (1 Kings 17:1). That is oath language.

Any prophecy should make *God* look good, not the prophet. If you disagree with what I have said and decide to say, "Thus says the Lord," you had better know *absolutely* what you are claiming—namely, that God has sworn an oath to you. When Elijah said, "As the LORD, the God of Israel, lives," it meant God swore an oath to him. If, therefore, you say, "The Lord told me," you had better get it right; otherwise, you are abusing His name.

Let's be honest. When people say, "The Lord told me," are they trying to make *God* look good? No. They are trying to make themselves look good—or at least they are hoping you will believe what they say if they claim it is "from the Lord."

Question: What if the Lord *did* give you a word? Good. I am thrilled for you, but do you need to tell anyone? What would be your motive in saying the *Lord* gave you this word? Would it be to make *Him* look good or to make *you* look good?

If you say, "My motive is to encourage people," I believe you, but what if that word does not come true? How often will you get away with this repeated claim: "The Lord says"? Loving caution: keep God's name out of it unless you would go to the stake for what you are claiming.

You can always say, "I feel I should share this word with you." If the word is genuinely from God, it will be recognized in due course; no need to rush it!

Are there exceptions to what I have urged in this chapter? I hope so! Perhaps you have heard the saying, "The exception that proves the rule." If so, I believe there are good prophetic people around who mean no harm when they say, "The Lord told me." When we lived in Key Largo, I took John Paul Jackson to meet my neighbors across the street. John Paul gave them the most encouraging word they could have heard. They asked, "How did you know to say this?"

He replied, "The Lord told me." In this case it honestly seemed to reassure them. What is more, even though John Paul set a time on his prophecy, which made me nervous, it turned out to be entirely accurate.

Another possible exception that comes to mind is Bobby Conner. He claims that Jesus talks to him all the time, and I am inclined to believe him. His words are almost always

Bible verses to people, and they have always been correct—so far as I can tell.

I am not saying, then, that you should never say, "The Lord told me" or "Thus says the Lord." I am urging you never to say it unless you have that oath-level assurance that God has spoken. Even then, you don't *have* to say it!

If you leave the Lord's name out, you won't regret it. You can always say, "I am compelled to share this with you," if you believe the Lord has spoken. You are also safe if the word is not from above. You will not be embarrassed, and you will not have abused God's name.

Remember, James said, "Above all" do not misuse the Lord's name "so that you may not fall under condemnation" (Jas. 5:12). Misusing His name isn't worth it.

Chapter Eleven

ISAAC

*And God said to Abraham, "As for Sarai you wife, you
shall not call her name Sarai, but Sarah shall be her
name. I will bless her, and moreover, I will give you a
son by her. I will bless her, and she shall become nations;
kings of peoples shall come from her." Then Abraham
fell on his face and laughed and said to himself, "Shall
a child be born to a man who is a hundred years old?
Shall Sarah, who is ninety years old, bear a child?"
And Abraham said to God, "Oh that Ishmael might
live before you!" God said, "No, but Sarah your wife
shall bear you a son, and you shall call his name
Isaac. I will establish my covenant with him as an
everlasting covenant for his offspring after him."*

—GENESIS 17:15–19

*For the earth will be filled with the knowledge of
the glory of the LORD as the waters cover the sea.*

—HABAKKUK 2:14

JONATHAN EDWARDS TAUGHT us that the task of every generation is to discover which direction the sovereign Redeemer is moving in, and move in that direction. One should also remember that Edwards—no doubt the leading light in America's Great Awakening of the eighteenth century—also thought that he was witnessing the prophecy of Habakkuk in his own day. It is sometimes called "the latter-day glory"—an era that will precede the second coming of Jesus. I join many people in church history who have believed that a major move of the Holy Spirit will encircle the globe before the end. Some of these understandably thought they were seeing this glory in their day. Like them, I believe we will witness it in our day. Time will tell if the essential teaching of this chapter is from the Lord.

I call this latter-day glory "Isaac." Abraham hoped the promised son would be Ishmael, but he had to adjust. Many Charismatics have thought the Pentecostal/Charismatic movement of the twentieth century was "it"—the final move of the Holy Spirit before the second coming of Jesus. I believe the best is yet to be: Isaac is coming.

My arrival at this point of view regarding Isaac was via a long process, beginning in the 1960s. When I was pastor of a church in Carlisle, Ohio, I read about the glossolalia movement in *Time* magazine. Before being known as the Charismatic movement, it was called glossolalia—from the Greek *glossa* for *tongue*—since the common denominator of the movement was largely speaking in tongues.

Lo and behold, one week later I was invited to a minister's luncheon in a nearby town where one of the main figures mentioned in the *Time* article was the guest speaker—a minister from the Reformed Church in America. He was indeed one of the best-known ministers in this movement at the time and became highly regarded by many. I went to hear him, and it happened that I was seated across the table from him.

As he was a minister in the Reformed Church, I asked if he was a Calvinist. Yes. He added that Loraine Boettner's (1901–1990) book *The Reformed Doctrine of Predestination* (P & R Publishing) had a major influence on him. This got my attention. I knew the book and the author. His talk to the ministers was impressive. He then invited those who desired prayer to receive the gift of tongues to stay behind. I told him that I had spoken in tongues a few years before. He said I could do it again.

I stayed to receive prayer. I knelt at the altar in this church and said, "Lord, if you are behind this, let it come; if not, stop it." I was utterly sincere and thought speaking in tongues would return. However, after he prayed for me, nothing happened. He then said, "Take the verse literally, 'Make a joyful noise to the LORD' [Ps. 100:1]."

I asked, "What do you mean?"

"Just make a joyful noise," he replied.

"I don't understand."

"Then just make a noise," he said with a bit of frustration.

"I don't understand."

"Just say, 'Ah.'"

"Ah," I dutifully replied.

"Well?" he inquired. "Do you feel anything?"

"No."

"Let's try again," he suggested. "Say, 'Ah.'"

Nothing happened when I said, "Ah," and by now he had lost me. I stood up, gave up, and went home. I unexpectedly ran into him the next day at a restaurant. He said to me, "I have been praying for you. You are the first not to have come through."

I have thought about that incident a thousand times. Rightly or wrongly, I formed an impression that stuck. I was uneasy with him trying—what seemed to me—to work something up. I was even more ill at ease to learn that it had worked every time before. It eventually made me wonder if the glossolalia movement, which later became known as the Charismatic movement, was something that man tried to cause to happen like Abraham sleeping with Hagar to make good God's promise to him.

A few years later Rolfe Barnard (1904–1969), one of my early Calvinist mentors, played a significant role in my grasp of Charismatics. Whereas many of Rolfe's fellow ministers and followers largely dismissed the Pentecostals and Charismatics from consideration as movements of God, Rolfe definitely had a different perspective. He believed God was in these movements. He was especially intrigued by David du Plessis (1905–1987), the South African Pentecostal.

However, Rolfe's verbatim comment regarding the Charismatic movement was: "I believe that God is in it, but that's not *it*." That was his way of saying there would be something much greater to come, namely, the "latter-day glory."

In the autumn of 1973, a few weeks after I arrived in Oxford, I went to hear du Plessis at a special meeting there.

I had learned that Smith Wigglesworth made a significant prophecy to du Plessis, and because Rolfe spoke favorably of him, I didn't want to miss it. I'm glad I went, but—to be candid—I found him more than a little disappointing. I expected more. Little he said rang true with me. I certainly agreed with Rolfe: "This is not *it*." Over the next several months I was gripped by the notion that the Charismatic movement could be compared to Ishmael and that Isaac represents the genuine latter-day glory.

Did I get this from the Lord? You tell me. I shared this first at my church in Lower Heyford, Oxfordshire. The members of Westminster Chapel will remember this comparison very well. I shared it with Dr. Lloyd-Jones. He did not commit to it but clearly liked the idea. If you put me under a lie detector, I would say it was from the Lord, but at the end of the day, we will have to wait and see what happens.

Never in my life had I known fear and trembling as I felt in the days before I originally gave this message at the Wembley Conference Centre in October 1992. My writing in this chapter is an elaboration of what I proposed on that evening.

I was forecasting a new era, one that can be called a post-Charismatic era.

When I use the term Charismatic, I see it as shorthand for the work of the Spirit—including with Pentecostals— that we've all known about throughout the past century.

A few days before the Word and Spirit Conference, Lyndon Bowring and I had a meal with a respected Charismatic leader. Quite spontaneously I put this question to him: "If the Charismatic movement is either Ishmael or Isaac, which do you think it is?"

He answered, "Isaac."

I said to him, "What if I told you that the Charismatic movement is not Isaac but Ishmael?"

His answer was, "I hope not."

This man, a Spirit-filled godly man, responded exactly as Abraham did: "And Abraham said to God, 'If only Ishmael might live under your blessing!'" (Gen. 17:18, NIV).

God was handing Abraham what he had wanted more than anything in the world—the promise of a son through his beloved wife, Sarah—and he was rejecting it! When God's promise was originally given, I'm sure Abraham would never have believed that one day he would react so negatively to something so positive.

That is largely the way many Charismatics reacted to my address that evening. The point that Isaac is coming—something more significant than we have ever seen—did not compensate for the pain they felt that night. "You call us Ishmael," a close Charismatic friend said to me. "But Isaac is coming," I stressed.

It was hard for some Charismatics to accept the notion that the movement they gave their lives for and endured persecution for was not "it" after all. I understood that. However, the same Charismatic friend I just quoted has since embraced my position. Indeed, now that it is more than twenty-five years later, Charismatics almost everywhere are saying to me, "We hope you are right. Because if what we now have is all there is, the future is pretty bleak."

ABRAHAM BELIEVED GOD'S WORD

For thirteen years Abraham sincerely believed that Ishmael was the promised son. It all began years earlier when he was given a promise from God. Indeed, believing that promise meant that righteousness was put to his credit.

> After these things the word of the LORD came to Abram in a vision: "Fear not, Abram, I am your shield; your reward shall be very great." But Abram said, "O Lord GOD, what will you give me, for I continue childless, and the heir of my house is Eliezer of Damascus?" And Abram said, "Behold, you have given me no offspring, and a member of my household will be my heir." And behold, the word of the LORD came to him: "This man shall not be your heir; your very own son shall be your heir." And he brought him outside and said, "Look toward heaven, and number the stars, if you are able to number them." Then he said to him, "So shall your offspring be." And he believed the LORD, and he counted it to him as righteousness.
>
> —GENESIS 15:1–6

Abraham might have said to God, "Do you expect me to believe that? You must be joking. I am eighty-five, and Sarah is seventy." But no, Abraham *believed* it. By believing the promise, righteousness was credited to Abraham. This became the apostle Paul's chief illustration for the doctrine of justification by faith (Rom. 4). It was what Martin Luther rediscovered in the sixteenth century, and it turned the world upside down.

Here is the Gospel in a nutshell: When we believe that Jesus died on the cross for our sins, and we transfer all the hope we once placed in our works onto what Jesus did for us on the cross, righteousness is put to our credit as though we had never sinned. That is the Gospel.

Abraham believed that promise, but the years were rolling by. No son. Sarah was getting older. No son. She was far past the age in which it was usually possible for a woman to bear a child. Abraham and Sarah were both discouraged. We all get discouraged when God delays the fulfillment of His word. We all tend to fret during the era of unanswered prayer. We all know the pain of waiting, having been sure that we got it right. Abraham was sure when God said that He would make his descendants as numerous as the stars in the sky (Gen. 15:5), but nothing was happening.

One day Sarah came up with a solution.

> Now Sarai, Abram's wife, had borne him no children. But she had an Egyptian slave named Hagar; so she said to Abram, "The LORD has kept me from having children. Go, sleep with my slave; perhaps I can build a family through her." Abram agreed to what Sarai said. So after Abram had been living in Canaan ten years, Sarai his wife took her Egyptian slave Hagar and gave her to her husband to be his wife. He slept with Hagar, and she conceived.
>
> —GENESIS 16:1–4, NIV

Abraham did not initiate this idea; it was entirely Sarah's. Why did he agree to it? Because Abraham really did believe the promise, and he was willing to see it happen any way God chose to bring it about. What is more, if Hagar's child happened to be a male, having come from Abraham's own body, it would fulfill the promise. That would give every reason to believe that God was at work. A male child would fit the promise of Genesis 15:4–5.

Hagar conceived, but Sarah had second thoughts.

> [Abram] went in to Hagar, and she conceived. And when she saw that she had conceived, she looked with contempt on her mistress. And Sarai said to Abram, "May the wrong done to me be on you! I gave my servant to your embrace, and when she saw that she had conceived, she looked on me with contempt. May the LORD judge between you and me!"
>
> —GENESIS 16:4–5

Hagar despised Sarah; Sarah persecuted Hagar. Hagar fled to the desert. An angel of the Lord visited her. He then announced to Hagar, "You are pregnant and shall bear a son. You shall call his name Ishmael, because the LORD has listened to your affliction" (Gen. 16:11).

We know four things at this stage:

1. Sarah persecuted Hagar.

2. God affirmed Hagar.

3. The child was male.

4. The seal of God was on Ishmael. Abraham could never forget this.

Ishmael was born when Abraham was eighty-six. As far as Abraham was concerned, God had kept His word. There could be no doubt about it. Everything pointed to Ishmael's being the promised son, and so Abraham said to God, "If only Ishmael might live under your blessing."

Abraham had not only become reconciled to the suggestion that Hagar should be the mother of his son, but he saw that it seemingly met every condition of the promise of Genesis 15:4—every condition he ever imagined. Genesis 15:4, as far as Abraham was concerned, was now ancient history—*it was done*. God had kept His word—that was that. Ishmael met the requirements, and Abraham had no complaints.

One day Abraham got up like on any other morning, unprepared for what would happen on that day. What a difference a day makes! Abraham was now ninety-nine years old, and Ishmael, his pride and joy, was a teenager. Never underestimate how much Abraham loved Ishmael, his one and only son. Then out of the blue, God appeared to Abraham.

> When Abram was ninety-nine years old the LORD appeared to Abram and said to him, "I am God Almighty; walk before me, and be blameless, that I may make my covenant between me and you, and may multiply you greatly." Then Abram fell on his face. And God said to him, "Behold, my covenant is with you, and you shall be the father of a multitude of nations. No longer shall your name be called Abram, but your name shall be Abraham."
>
> —GENESIS 17:1–5

So far Abraham enjoyed every word that he heard on that day. God gave him the covenant of circumcision, the incredible promise that he would be the father of many nations; the land of Canaan would be an everlasting possession; he loved every moment of it. Everything was going fine with Abraham.

Moreover, no problem about the circumcision—Abraham would circumcise Ishmael and would himself be circumcised. The covenant would extend to his household, even to foreigners who became a part of his household. The covenant was inflexible—not to keep it was to forfeit the promise. That was fine. So far, so good.

Then came some news for which Abraham was unprepared. It ought to have been the grandest, most sublime, most fantastic promise that his ears would ever hear. However, he couldn't believe what he was hearing, and he didn't like it.

> And God said to Abraham, "As for Sarai your wife, you shall not call her name Sarai, but Sarah shall be her name. I will bless her, and moreover, I will give you a son by her. I will bless her, and she shall become nations; kings of peoples shall come from her." Then Abraham fell on his face and laughed and said to himself, "Shall a child be born to a man who is a hundred years old? Shall Sarah, who is ninety years old, bear a child?" And Abraham said to God, "Oh that Ishmael might live before you!"
>
> —Genesis 17:15–18

Abraham's world was now turned upside down. He was uttering an impassioned, painful plea, "Please let the covenant be fulfilled in Ishmael."

I am prepared to say that this is precisely what God is saying to us at the present time. Sarah, whom the apostle Paul called "the mother of us all," will conceive. For all I know, she has already conceived. Someone said that Isaac will be an "ugly baby" but a handsome man when he comes of age. The hidden, sovereign work of the Holy Spirit often emerges in the least likely people and places. However much we love Ishmael—the Pentecostal and Charismatic movement—however much God affirmed Ishmael, and however much Ishmael fit what many hoped for, God is up to something new. God was behind Ishmael, but Ishmael is not God's ultimate purpose. Sarah will conceive. Isaac will show up any day.

I now return to my friend who hoped that the Charismatic movement was Isaac. I said to him, "Why should this make you so sad? When we consider what God is up to next, that it will be far greater—as Isaac was to Ishmael—what will it be like when God does something unprecedented in the land? If Ishmael could give Abraham so much joy, how much more Isaac? If Ishmael was blessed by God, how much more Isaac?"

Today when we consider how God has blessed the Church through the Charismatic and Pentecostal movements, and how many wonderful and thrilling things have come during this era, what will Isaac be like?

WHY SHOULD THE PENTECOSTAL-CHARISMATIC ERA BE AFFIRMED?

Abraham did not initiate the era of Ishmael. He was an honorable man who believed God's promise. Sarah, the mother of us all, was the instigator of the whole thing, and we should honor her. The promise of a son came to Abraham as a word from God. Furthermore, God's affirmation of Ishmael to Hagar proves it was of God.

The Charismatic era is of God. He did it, and we're all the better for it. Most churches worth their salt today in the United Kingdom—England, Wales, Scotland, and Northern Ireland—are charismatic. Whereas in the United Kingdom the Charismatic movement is mainstream, such is seen in the United States as the lunatic fringe. This is all the more reason there is a stigma in the United States against upholding all the gifts of the Spirit.

The greatest hymnody that the last one hundred years have seen has emerged from the Charismatic movement. From Graham Kendrick to Matt Redman to Hillsong, where would we be today without their contribution? When you consider that the widespread revival, particularly in Africa, Latin America, South America, Indonesia, and Korea, is largely Pentecostal, you can see why we should affirm the Charismatic era.

Sarah persecuted Hagar. Consider how much Charismatics and Pentecostals have suffered, mainly from Evangelicals! Pentecostals, neo-Pentecostals, those who dare talk about the gifts of the Spirit, signs, wonders, and miracles, have been "outside the camp"—like Hagar in the desert. They have been put down, lied about, misunderstood, and persecuted as much as those in any era in the history of the Christian church.

An undoubted divine visitation affirmed Hagar in the desert. She could look up to God through her tears. I love the way the King James Version puts it; it moves me almost to tears every time I read it: Hagar "called the name of the LORD that spake unto her, Thou God seest me" (Gen. 16:13). Hagar knew that God had given her a son. God even gave the son the name Ishmael, which means "God hears."[1] God left Hagar in no doubt that He was with her, that He was behind it all. Likewise, those who unashamedly regard themselves as Charismatics know that God has visited them; God has affirmed them. They have seen the supernatural. My heart warms to them; they are among my closest friends; I am one of them.

It is not all worked up. Undoubted signs and wonders have characterized Pentecostals and Charismatics all over the world. It is sad that much of the Charismatic movement has allowed prosperity teaching to replace the supernatural.

Furthermore, God had a secret purpose for Ishmael that was revealed first to Hagar and later to Abraham.

> The angel of the LORD also said to [Hagar], "I will surely multiply your offspring so that they cannot be numbered for multitude."
>
> —GENESIS 16:10

> As for Ishmael, I have heard you; behold, I have blessed him and will make him fruitful and multiply him greatly. He shall father twelve princes,

and I will make him into a great nation. But I will
establish my covenant with Isaac.
                                    —GENESIS 17:20–21

We haven't seen the end of this yet, by the way. The
natural, literal, Arabic descendants of Ishmael are too
numerous to count. They have spread in ever-increasing
numbers, and their mosques and places of worship are
going up rapidly in every major city. Who knows what the
end will be? We are going to see Islam turning to Christ
before it is all over. "No eye has seen, nor ear heard, nor
the heart of man imagined, what God has prepared for
those who love him—these things God has revealed to us
through the Spirit" (1 Cor. 2:9–10).

THE POST-CHARISMATIC ERA

Now I want to show first why Ishmael was not meant to be
the promised child. God wanted the promise of the Gospel
as revealed to Abraham to be fulfilled in a manner that
defied a natural explanation. Conversion is the greatest
miracle that can happen under the sun. It is a sovereign
work of God; it is what God does. When Hagar conceived,
it was natural, but when Sarah conceived, it defied a natural explanation; only God could have done it.

God wanted the heirs of the Gospel to look back on what
He did in a manner no one would question. Understandable
though it was for Abraham to agree with Sarah's proposal,
there would always be a cloud over it. Even Abraham must
have questioned, "Was sleeping with Hagar the right thing
to do? Is this all there is? Is this really what God had in
mind when He gave the promise?"

I don't mean to be unfair, but although the presence of the supernatural cannot be denied, one must admit that the real, undoubted, empirical proof of signs and wonders is not all that common in recent years. As I said earlier, I believe this is why prosperity teaching has largely replaced healing as the emphasis of an ever-increasing number of prominent Charismatics and Pentecostals, especially in America. But genuine miracles are being seen in third world countries. I witnessed a deaf and mute woman speak the name "Jesus" in the bush in Mozambique, Africa, when Heidi Baker prayed for her.

HOW WILL ISAAC APPEAR?

Isaac will appear suddenly when the church generally is in a deep sleep, expecting nothing. There are at least two occurrences in Scripture that point to the same thing.

1. The prophecy of Malachi

> I send my messenger, and he will prepare the way before me. And the Lord whom you seek will suddenly come to his temple; and the messenger of the covenant in whom you delight, behold, he is coming, says the LORD of hosts. But who can endure the day of his coming, and who can stand when he appears? For he is like a refiner's fire and like fullers' soap. He will sit as a refiner and purifier of silver, and he will purify the sons of Levi and refine them like gold and silver, and they will bring offerings in righteousness to the LORD. Then the offering of Judah and Jerusalem will be

pleasing to the LORD as in the days of old and as
in former years.

—MALACHI 3:1–4

Although John the Baptist himself fulfilled Malachi's
prophecy, the latter part of Malachi's word above says that
the Jews and Jerusalem will be pleasing to the Lord "as
in the days of old and as in former years." *That was not
the case* when Jesus came on the scene. They rejected Him.
The references to Levi and Judah and Jerusalem are therefore *unfulfilled*. Instead of the Jews in Jerusalem pleasing
the Lord, the opposite was true. Jesus wept over Jerusalem
because they forfeited what belonged to them, owing to
their rejection of their promised Messiah.

> O Jerusalem, Jerusalem, the city that kills the
> prophets and stones those who are sent to it! How
> often would I have gathered your children together
> as a hen gathers her brood under her wings, and
> you were not willing! See, your house is left to
> you desolate. For I tell you, you will not see me
> again, until you say, "Blessed is he who comes in
> the name of the Lord."
>
> —MATTHEW 23:37–39

Would that you, even you, had known on this day
the things that make for peace! But now they are
hidden from your eyes. For the days will come
upon you, when your enemies will set up a bar-
ricade around you and surround you and hem you
in on every side and tear you down to the ground,
you and your children within you. And they will

> not leave one stone upon another in you, because
> you did not know the time of your visitation.
>
> —LUKE 19:42–44

In other words, Malachi's prophecy that the Jews and Jerusalem would please the Lord must still be future! However, I will add: Isaac will be a John the Baptist type ministry. As John the Baptist prepared the way for Jesus, Isaac—when the Word and the Spirit reunite—will get the bride of Christ ready for the second coming of Jesus.

2. The parable of the ten virgins

> But at midnight [Greek *middle of night*] there was
> a cry, "Here is the bridegroom! Come out to meet
> him." Then all those virgins rose and trimmed
> their lamps. And the foolish said to the wise,
> "Give us some of your oil, for our lamps are going
> out." But the wise answered, saying, "Since there
> will not be enough for us and for you, go rather to
> the dealers and buy for yourselves."
>
> —MATTHEW 25:6–9

Picture yourself at 2:00 a.m. The last thing you want is to be awakened at that hour. Jesus said that in the very last days the church will be aptly described as *asleep*. I deal with this in *Prepare Your Heart for the Midnight Cry*. When the church generally is decadent, powerless, asleep, and expecting nothing, Isaac will appear.

There will be three categories of Christians at that time: (1) the wise sleeping virgins, (2) the foolish sleeping virgins, and (3) those who actually wake up the church to say, "Here is the Bridegroom! Come out to meet Him." This third category will be comprised of a remnant *not asleep* but available to God the Holy Spirit to wake up the church in the last days.

As one prophetic person put it a few years ago: "There is a resurgence of the fear of the Lord coming, and it will fall suddenly, unexpectedly, and unannounced. A new day is coming; it is not an encore—this will be like no other. This will be a hallmark of a huge wave of the Spirit that will sweep around the earth. It will be about holiness and purity of heart. It is a waste of time telling folk to get ready. It will just come. Suddenly. A revival with a hallmark of tears, but also profound intimacy with the person of the Holy Spirit."[2]

This prophetic word coheres with the prophecy in Malachi 3:1–4.

WHAT ISAAC WILL LOOK LIKE

A restoration of the Gospel

My late friend John Paul Jackson told me of his vision of what I am calling Isaac. He said that the key to the next great move of God on the earth would be the Book of Romans, especially chapter 4. This means that history will repeat itself. Romans 4 is about justification by faith alone. As I show in *Whatever Happened to the Gospel?*, this is the message that turned the world upside down in Martin Luther's day. It is what gave John Wesley his heartwarming experience in Aldersgate Street in London in 1738. As I said earlier, Wesley taught Whitefield the teaching of justification by faith. It was the key to Jonathan Edwards' preaching in the years that led to the Great Awakening in his day.

In the previously mentioned scenario, one might overlook what the promise of Isaac eventually did for Abraham: it drove him back to God's word. In Romans chapter 4 the apostle Paul, having dealt with Genesis 15:6, shows the basis of his doctrine of justification by faith; he suddenly jumps to the time when Abraham was reconciled to the fact that Isaac was on the way.

> Against all hope, Abraham in hope believed and so became the father of many nations, just as it had been said to him, "So shall your offspring be." Without weakening in his faith, he faced the fact that his body was as good as dead—since he was about a hundred years old—and that Sarah's womb was also dead. Yet he did not waver through unbelief regarding the promise of God, but was strengthened in his faith and gave glory to God, being fully persuaded that God had power to do what he had promised. This is why "it was credited to him as righteousness."
>
> —ROMANS 4:18–22, NIV

It was credited to Abraham as righteousness when he believed the first time. But now he is believing again, and he goes back to God's original promise. Abraham now has something to live for that exceeds his greatest expectation. For over the years, Abraham had underestimated the word—the dignity of it, the glory of it. But with the promise of Isaac on the way, once he became reconciled to what God said was going to happen next, it drove him back to the word.

The coming of Isaac will get the church back to the Word of God as we have not done for years. There will be a new romance with the Scriptures. It will be like falling in love all over again. It will result in a fresh assurance, a burst of power, and an expectancy that we never dreamed possible. We will have something to live for, unlike anything we have ever known.

A restoration of the fear of God

The coming of Isaac will be characterized by an awe of God and His Word not seen in our generation. "Who can endure the day of his coming, and who can stand when he appears?" (Mal. 3:2). A renewal of the fear of God will mean a return to holiness. Whatever happened to holiness? "He is like a refiner's fire and the fullers' soap" (Mal. 3:2). When the Word and the Spirit coalesce, it will be a re-marriage of what should never have separated. As with human marriage, God said, "What therefore God has joined together, let not man separate" (Matt. 19:6).

What then will Isaac look like? It will be an era in which the Word preached will be as awesome as the vindication of God's name—which means authentic signs, wonders, and miracles. It will be an era in which signs and wonders will not be under a cloud of suspicion but open to the minutest scrutiny. As the New Testament skeptics said of the miracle of the disabled man who suddenly was walking, "We cannot deny it" (Acts 4:16).

Islamic people turning to Christ and the lifting of the blindness on Israel

Millions of Muslims will be converted. Thousands of Muslims who have had dreams about Jesus will come out of hiding. This will include imams who are at the moment afraid to discuss this. This phenomenon will dazzle the world.

At the moment, it is virtually impossible to get very far in presenting the Gospel to a Jew. In Israel it is forbidden for a Christian to evangelize. But something—I am not sure what—will cause the light to turn on in the hearts of Jews from all parts of the world. They will be a part of an evangelism effort that leads Jews, Muslims, and people of all races and nations to Christ.

It will be an era when the Gospel, as well as signs and wonders, will be at the forefront of priorities among God's ministers. It will be an era when conversion to Christ will not be minimized but seen as the greatest miracle that can happen. It will be an era in which the most difficult cases imaginable will turn into putty in the hands of a sovereign God; when surprising conversions become common. Some of those who have opposed the Gospel the most, have laughed at biblical infallibility, and have dismissed the historic Christian faith will fall on their faces before God in repentance. It will be an era when the world will fear the prayers of God's people more than they fear nuclear war. Mary Queen of Scots is said to have feared John Knox's prayers "more than all the assembled armies."[3]

The post-Charismatic era will be a time when government and people in high places will come on bended knee to God's people and ask for help. With Ishmael it was the promise of a nation; with Isaac it was the promise of many nations. The apostle Paul said that Isaac is the "heir of the world" (Rom. 4:13). We're talking about something big. We're talking about something that is wider than one nation's boundaries, when kings of the earth, leaders of nations, are made to see that there is a God in the heavens. It will be an era in which children will be sovereign vessels, an age when ordinary Christians are equipped with prophetic gifts. It won't be a case of religious superstars vying for TV time, trying to be seen or heard, or trying to prove themselves. We're talking about an awakening that reaches forgotten areas, cuts into people's hearts, and turns upside down places that heretofore were thought to be impenetrable. All this will come without the aid of the media, public relations firms, or the endorsement of high-profile celebrities.

The coming of Isaac will begin an era in which the glory of the Lord covers the earth as the waters cover the sea.

Smith Wigglesworth is alleged to have made a prophecy three months before he died that forecast a coming together of the Word and Spirit. This is what he reportedly said:

> During the next few decades there will be two distinct moves of the Holy Spirit across the church and Great Britain. The first move will affect every church that is open to receive it and will be characterized by a restoration of the baptism and gifts of the Holy Spirit. The second move of the Holy Spirit will result in people leaving historic churches and planting new churches. In the duration of each of these moves, the people who are involved will say, "This is the great revival." But

the Lord says "No, neither is this the great revival but both are steps towards it."

When the new church phase is on the wane, there will be evidenced in the churches something that has not been seen before: a coming together of those with an emphasis on the Word and those with an emphasis on the Spirit.

When the Word and the Spirit come together, there will be the biggest movement of the Holy Spirit that the nation, and indeed the world, has ever seen. It will mark the beginning of a revival that will eclipse anything that has been witnessed within these shores, even the Wesleyan and the Welsh revivals of former years. The outpouring of God's Spirit will flow over from the UK to the mainland of Europe, and from there will begin a missionary move to the ends of the earth.[4]

Even if Wigglesworth had not said that, I believe that the next thing to happen on God's calendar is not the second coming but the awakening of the church before the end. How long will this era last? I don't know.

The Lord said: "Write down the revelation...so that a herald may run with it. For the revelation awaits an appointed time; it speaks of the end and will not prove false. Though it linger, wait for it; it will certainly come and will not delay" (Hab. 2:2–3, NIV).

"O that Ishmael might live under your blessing!" begged Abraham, but God said Isaac would be the one. The name Isaac means he laughs. As at Pentecost when mocking turned to fear, the Word and Spirit coming together will bring about an era when cynical laughter will turn to reverent fear and joy.

CONCLUSION

I said near the beginning of this book that much of the preaching I have done in my lifetime—if I am utterly candid—was "Word only." When people came to Westminster Chapel, they did not expect to *see* things happen; they came to *hear* the Word. Conversely, there are churches where people go not so much to *hear* but to *see* things happen. Who can blame them?

Jesus, however, could dazzle the multitudes with the power of His word as easily as when He performed miracles. The people were astonished when He spoke and astonished when He healed. The simultaneous combination of the Word and the Spirit in great and equal measure will do that. And when this takes place, as my friend Lyndon Bowring puts it, "Those who come to see will hear, and those who come to hear will see."

May God the Father, Son, and Holy Spirit bless you and keep you now and evermore. Amen.

NOTES

Chapter One
Can We Have the Word Without the Spirit?

1.   Blue Letter Bible, *"parrēsia,"* accessed April 22, 2019, https://www.blueletterbible.org//lang/lexicon/lexicon.cfm?Strongs=g3954&t=kjv.

2.   This is a typical saying used by Jack Taylor, with whom I often preach.

Chapter Two
Being on Good Terms With the Holy Spirit

1.   As cited in Marva J. Dawn, *Morning by Morning* (Grand Rapids, MI: Eerdmans, 2001), 242. A variant appears on page 280 of John R. Rice's *Prayer* (Murfreesboro, TN: Sword of the Lord Publishers, 1970): "Martin Luther said that he had so much work to do for God that he could never get it done unless he prayed three hours a day!" Neither author cites a source for this saying.

Chapter Three
How to Get More of the Holy Spirit

1.   Charles Wesley, "Love Divine, All Loves Excelling," 1747, https://hymnary.org/text/love_divine_all_love_excelling_joy_of_he.

2.   Joseph Medlicott Scriven, "What a Friend We Have in Jesus," 1855, https://hymnary.org/text/what_a_friend_we_have_in_jesus_all_our_s.

3.   Dwight L. Moody, as quoted in *Rick Warren's Bible Study Methods* (Grand Rapids, MI: Zondervan, 2006), 16.

4.   "Longest Ongoing Pilgrimage," Guinness World Records Limited, April 24, 2013, http://www.guinnessworldrecords.com/world-records/longest-ongoing-pilgrimage.

Chapter Four
The Fruit of the Spirit

1.   Frances R. Havergal, "Like a River Glorious," 1876, https://library.timelesstruths.org/music/Like_a_River_Glorious/.

2.   Blue Letter Bible, s.v. "*praÿtēs*," accessed April 23, 2019, https://www.blueletterbible.org/lang/lexicon/lexicon.cfm?Strongs=G4240&t=ESV.

3.   Blue Letter Bible, s.v. "*egkrateia*," accessed April 23, 2019, https://www.blueletterbible.org//lang/lexicon/lexicon.cfm?Strongs=g1466&t=kjv.

Chapter Five
The Gifts of the Spirit

1.   Blue Letter Bible, s.v. *"zēloō,"* accessed April 23, 2019, https://www.blueletterbible.org//lang/lexicon/lexicon.cfm?Strongs=g2206&t=kjv.

2.   Blue Letter Bible, s.v. *"sophia,"* accessed April 23, 2019, https://www.blueletterbible.org//lang/lexicon/lexicon.cfm?Strongs=g4678&t=kjv.

3.   Blue Letter Bible, s.v. *"oida,"* accessed April 23, 2019, https://www.blueletterbible.org//lang/lexicon/lexicon.cfm?Strongs=g6063&t=esv.

4.   Bible Hub, s.v. *"charisma,"* accessed April 23, 2019, https://biblehub.com/greek/5486.htm.

Chapter Six
Can We Have the Spirit Without the Word?

1.   A. W. Tozer, *God's Pursuit of Man* (Chicago: Moody Publishers, 2015), 16.

2.   William Rees, "Here Is Love," stanzas 1–2, 1855; trans. by William Edwards, 1915; stanza 3 attributed to William Williams, 1744, https://hymnary.org/text/here_is_love_vast_as_the_ocean/fulltexts.

3.   Frances Crosby, "Pass Me Not, O Gentle Savior," 1868, https://library.timelesstruths.org/music/Pass_Me_Not_O_Gentle_Savior/.

4.   In communication with author.

Chapter Seven
Logos and Rhema

1.   J. Harrison Hudson, "The Impact of Robert Murray M'Cheyne," *Life and Work*, January 1987, https://www.mcheyne.info/harrison-hudson.php.

Chapter Eight
The Silent Divorce

1.   R. T. Kendall, *Tithing* (Grand Rapids, MI: Zondervan, 1982), 20.

2.   I learned of this from a personal conversation with someone who witnessed it firsthand.

3.   I learned of this in a personal conversation and confirmed it with the preacher's staff members.

4.   "Faith alone plus nothing" is a phrase I learned from the late Francis Schaeffer (1912–1984).

5.   As quoted in John Fowles, *The Journals Volume One* (Evanston, IL: Northwestern University Press, 2003), 581.

Chapter Nine
Where Promises and Power Meet

1.   *Encyclopaedia Britannica*, s.v. "Phillip Brooks," accessed April 25, 2019, https://www.britannica.com/biography/Phillips-Brooks.

2.   Blue Letter Bible, s.v. *"chrisma,"* accessed April 25, 2019, https://www.blueletterbible.org//lang/lexicon/lexicon.cfm?Strongs=g5545&t=kjv.

3.   Blue Letter Bible, s.v. *"chriō,"* accessed April 22, 2019, https://www.blueletterbible.org//lang/lexicon/lexicon.cfm?Strongs=G5548&t=KJV; Blue Letter Bible, s.v. *"Christos,"* accessed April 29, 2019, https://www.blueletterbible.org/lang/lexicon/lexicon.cfm?Strongs=G5547&t=KJV.

4.   Blue Letter Bible, s.v. *"apophtheggomai,"* accessed April 22, 2019, https://www.blueletterbible.org//lang/lexicon/lexicon.cfm?Strongs=G669&t=KJV.

5.   Blue Letter Bible, s.v. *"chriō."*

6.   Matthew L. G. Zickler, "Luther and Calvin," The Lutheran Church—Missouri Synod, June 14, 2017, https://lutheranreformation.org/theology/luther-and-calvin.

7.   Mike Puma, "Leader of Men," ESPN Classic, accessed April 25, 2019, http://www.espn.com/classic/biography/s/Lombardi_Vince.html.

8.   Charles Spurgeon, *The Complete Works of C. H. Spurgeon* (Harrington, DE: Delmarva Publications Inc., 2015).

9.   Wikisource, s.v. "Heralds of God/Chapter 2," last modified March 13, 2014, 21:21, https://en.wikisource.org/w/index.php?title=Heralds_of_God/Chapter_2&oldid=4814208.

10.   Aristotle, *Rhetoric*, trans. W. Rhys Roberts (n.p.: Arcadia ebook, 2016), https://books.google.com/books?id=LNr9CwAAQBAJ&.

Chapter Ten
Prophetic Responsibility

1.   Blue Letter Bible, s.v. *"analogia,"* accessed April 26, 2019, https://www.blueletterbible.org//lang/lexicon/lexicon.cfm?Strongs=g356&t=kjv.

Chapter Eleven
Isaac

1.   Bible Hub, s.v. "Yishmael," accessed April 26, 2019, https://biblehub.com/hebrew/3458.htm.

2.   Paul Cain, "A Resurgence of the Fear of the Lord Is Coming!," Elijah List, February 13, 2018, http://www.elijahlist.com/words/display_word.html?ID=19670.

3.   As quoted in David Brody and Scott Lamb, *The Faith of Donald J. Trump* (New York: HarperCollins, 2018), 21.

4.   Smith Wigglesworth gave this prophecy in 1947.